NÚÑEZ

MATT & TOM OLDFIELD

ULTIMATE FOOTBALL HEROES

NÚÑEZ

FROM THE PLAYGROUND
TO THE PITCH

DINO

First published by Dino Books in 2024,
an imprint of Bonnier Books UK,
4th Floor, Victoria House, Bloomsbury Square, London WC1B 4DA
Owned by Bonnier Books,
Sveavägen 56, Stockholm, Sweden

X @UFHbooks
X @footieheroesbks
www.heroesfootball.com
www.bonnierbooks.co.uk

Paperback ISBN: 978 1 78946 791 8
E-book ISBN: 978 1 78946 798 7

British Library cataloguing-in-publication data:
A catalogue record for this book is available from the British Library.

Printed and bound in Great Britain by Clays Ltd, Elcograf S.p.A.

1 3 5 7 9 10 8 6 4 2

MIX
Paper | Supporting
responsible forestry
FSC
www.fsc.org   FSC® C018072

For Noah, Nico, Arlo and Lila

Matt Oldfield is a children's author focusing on the wonderful world of football. His other books include *Unbelievable Football* (winner of the 2020 Children's Sports Book of the Year) and the *Johnny Ball: Football Genius* series. In association with his writing, Matt also delivers writing workshops in schools.

Cover illustration by Dan Leydon.
To learn more about Dan, visit danleydon.com
To purchase his artwork visit etsy.com/shop/footynews
Or just follow him on X @danleydon

TABLE OF CONTENTS

ACKNOWLEDGEMENTS

First of all I'd like to thank everyone at Bonnier Books for supporting me and for running the ever-expanding UFH ship so smoothly. Writing stories for the next generation of football fans is both an honour and a pleasure. Thanks also to my agent, Nick Walters, for helping to keep my dream job going, year after year.

Next up, an extra big cheer for all the teachers, booksellers and librarians who have championed these books, and, of course, for the readers. The success of this series is truly down to you.

Okay, onto friends and family. I wouldn't be writing this series if it wasn't for my brother Tom. I owe him so much and I'm very grateful for his belief in me as an author. I'm also very grateful to the rest of my family, especially Mel, Noah, Nico and of course Mum and Dad. To my parents, I owe my biggest passions: football and books. They're a real inspiration for everything I do.

Thanks also go to my friends for all the love and laughs, but sorry, no I won't be getting 'a real job' anytime soon!

And finally, to Iona. I couldn't have done any of this without your encouragement and understanding. Much love to you, and to Arlo, Lila and Claude.

CHAPTER 1

KLOPP'S AGENT OF CHAOS

2nd March 2024, The City Ground, Nottingham

As Darwin stood on the touchline waiting to come on, he closed his eyes and clenched his fists.

'I can do this,' he told himself. He was determined to be Liverpool's super sub again, making a difference for his team when it mattered most. With his explosive pace and power, Darwin was the perfect man for the job, and he had already saved the day many times before:

Against Newcastle early in the season, with two late goals to turn the game around,

In the Merseyside Derby against Everton, where he

set up Mo Salah to secure the victory,

And against Brentford a few weeks before, when he scored with a cheeky chip on the counter-attack.

Now, could he become Liverpool's late hero again, away at Nottingham Forest? The score was still 0–0, and he had 30 minutes to grab a winning goal and keep his team at the top of the Premier League table.

Challenge accepted!

Although he wasn't always the most graceful footballer to watch, Darwin was a striker who could cause all kinds of problems for defenders, especially when they were tired towards the end of matches. He was tall, he was strong, he was super-speedy, and you never quite knew what he was going to do next: lose the ball, or play a killer pass; miss an open goal, or score an absolute worldie. That was exactly why his manager Jürgen Klopp had called on him: to be his agent of chaos.

Vamooooooooooos!

What an instant impact! From the moment he entered the field, Darwin changed the game completely with his energy and aggression. He didn't stop moving: left, right, centre; forward and back, all across the Liverpool forward line, and the ball seemed attracted to him like a magnet. Again and again, he got himself into dangerous positions and when the pass or cross arrived, there was only ever one thing on his mind: go for goal! Darwin was famous for taking far more shots than any other striker in the Premier League.

First, he fired wide with his left foot from a very tight angle,

Then he headed just wide from the centre of the box,

And then he had a long-range strike blocked by a defender.

Nearly! He was getting closer and closer, but unfortunately so was the final whistle. As the stadium clock ticked past 90 minutes, Liverpool were still searching for a winning goal. Darwin kept moving busily around the box, confident that a big chance would come his way eventually...

As a late corner came in from the left, Darwin made a clever run to the near post and leapt up high to meet it. Was this it; his match-winning moment? *FLICK!* His header deflected off a Forest defender and flew towards the bottom corner, but the keeper reacted brilliantly to make the save.

'Noooooooooooo!' Darwin groaned, with his hands on his head. So close! Oh well, hopefully there was still just enough time for another big chance to arrive...

In the 99th minute, Alexis Mac Allister won the ball back on the edge of the Forest penalty area and looked up to curl one last ball into the crowded box. Just as he pulled his left leg back, Darwin made his move in the middle, bursting in between two defenders. Surely, this was it – his second big chance to score.

Ooooooooooooooooooohhhh...

At first, the cross looked like it might float just over his head, but no, somehow Darwin managed to raise himself even higher and then swivel his head around to flick the ball down, into the bottom corner. *1–0!*

... Hurrrraaaaaaaaaaaaaayyyyy!

Goooooooooooooooooooooooooaaaaaaaaaaaaaaaaaa aaaaaaaaaallllllllllllllllllllllllllllllllllll!!!!!!!!!!!!!!!!

Whoa, Darwin had done it – he had saved the day for Liverpool yet again! As the fans went wild, he made a heart with his hands, and then slid towards the corner flag on his knees. What a feeling!

'Yessssssssssss!' he roared, like the big lion tattoo on his back. It was his 10th league goal of the season and his most significant by far. Thanks to him, Liverpool were staying at the top of the Premier League table.

'You hero!' Klopp cheered as he gave Darwin a big, happy hug after the final whistle. 'You deserve that moment, you really do.'

Since his big-money move from Benfica to Liverpool, Darwin had experienced many lows as well as highs, but no matter how many golden chances he missed, or how many angry comments he received on social media, he always kept going: listening, learning and working hard to improve.

Yes, for all his pace and power on the pitch, Darwin's positive mentality was perhaps his greatest weapon of all. Time and time again throughout his young life, he had shown the inner strength to bounce back – from bad injuries and bad form; from difficult starts and huge disappointments.

Darwin was a fighter with a big football dream, and he always had been, ever since his difficult early days in Artigas, Uruguay.

CHAPTER 2

HARD TIMES IN ARTIGAS

As he watched the water levels rise higher and higher all around them, Bibiano Núñez sighed and muttered to himself, 'Arghhh, not again!'

When Bibiano and Silvia had got married and started building their family home a few years earlier, brick by brick, room by room, they had known the main problem with living in El Pirata: flooding. Their neighbourhood sat right on the side of the Quaraí/ Cuareim River, which separated their country, Uruguay, from Brazil next door. And whenever there was really heavy rain, like there had been that year, the river burst its banks and flooded the poor people of El Pirata.

It was far from a perfect place to live, but what choice did they have? The Núñez family couldn't afford to move to a nicer, safer part of the city of Artigas. Bibiano worked long, difficult days as a builder, while Silvia cleaned houses and collected empty milk bottles from the streets to earn some extra money, but even then it was still a struggle to put enough food on the family table. Often, they had to go to bed hungry so that their two young sons, Junior and Darwin, could eat. And now, on top of all their other troubles, they were being forced out of their home... again.

After taking a long, deep breath, Bibiano went back inside to tell his family the bad news.

'Sorry, we've got to get out of here NOW – the floods are coming. Quickly grab a few of your favourite things, and then let's go!'

With heavy hearts, the boys rushed off to do as they were told. They didn't have many toys to take, but they did have favourite things that they really couldn't leave behind. For Junior, it was his football boots, and for his younger brother, it was his football.

It was the best present ever, and Little Darwin took it absolutely everywhere with him. If it wasn't tucked under his arm or glued to his feet, it was in the back of his old tricycle, or cuddled next to him at night.

'No Mum, leave it there,' he mumbled sleepily if Silvia ever tried to take it out of the bed. So of course there was no way that Darwin could go to stay at his grandparents' house for weeks or maybe even months without it.

'Got it – I'm ready to go!'

'Good boy. Now, can you help your mother with the bags?'

Their dad was a big football fan too, but it was Junior who had first introduced Darwin to the beautiful game. His brother was five years older than him and, ever since the day he learned to walk, Darwin had always wanted to go wherever Junior went, and do whatever Junior did:

Shopping,

'Hey, can I come too?'

School,

'Hey, can I go too?'

And especially football.

'Hey, can I play too? Pleeeeaaaaaasssssse!'

'OK, fiiiiiiiiiiine – just for a bit until my friends arrive...'

And from his very first kicks in the wild, grassy fields of El Pirata, Darwin had been hooked. Football was just so fun and exciting, even when it was just the two of them passing the ball back and forth, and the buzz he got when he finally fired a shot past his brother and scored a goal? No words could describe that feeling! Yes, from the very beginning, Darwin knew that he wanted to play football forever.

That was the plan for both brothers, in fact. Junior was already shining for local club San Miguel, and just like everything else in life, Darwin couldn't wait to follow in his footsteps. Together, they were going to take on the football world, and become famous superstars! Then, they would be able to buy a big new home for their parents, in a place that would never flood, and their hard times in Artigas would just be a distant memory in the past.

CHAPTER 3

THE BRILLIANT
NÚÑEZ BROTHERS

'OK, let's play first to five goals,' Junior announced with his hands on his hips and Darwin's favourite football trapped under his right foot. 'The loser has to do ALL the washing up after dinner. For a whole week!'

'Deal!' Darwin replied with a determined smile. 'I should get to start with the ball, though, because I'm the youngest.'

'Fine, but don't expect me to go easy on you, bro... '

After spending weeks with their grandparents while Bibiano fixed all the flood damage, the Núñez family was finally back in their house in El Pirata, and Junior and Darwin were finally back out on their favourite football pitch. Hurray! Soon, lots of other local kids would arrive and the real games would begin, but while they waited, why not warm up with a quick 1-vs-1 brother battle?

As the taller, stronger and older of the two of them, Junior was still the favourite, but he no longer felt as confident of victory as he used to. What his little brother lacked in size, he now more than made up for in skill, speed and will to win. These days, Darwin never seemed to stop playing football. If he wasn't scoring goal after goal in the playground at la Escuela Nº 56 Eladio F. Dieste, then he was out battling for the ball with the bigger kids in the local fields after school. The more he practised, the smaller the football gap between the brilliant Núñez brothers got, and the more competitive their contests became.

But while Junior was quietly very proud of Darwin's progress, he also had his own football pride to think about. For years, he had been seen as El Pirata's best young player, but now that title was in danger of being taken away... and handed to his little brother instead! If Junior lost, it would be the most humiliating thing EVER, so he was willing to do whatever it took to stop that from happening…

Darwin dribbled towards his big brother at speed, faking to go one way and then the other, but *BOOM!* With a barge of his shoulder, Junior knocked him over, stole the ball, and fired a shot between the rocks that served as goalposts. *1–0!*

In the past, Darwin might have sat there on the grass for ages, furiously screaming 'FOUL!' as tears streamed down his face, but not anymore. What was the point? There wasn't a single person watching them play, let alone an actual referee! All he could do was get up and go again…

As he dribbled towards his big brother, Darwin made his move earlier this time, but when he dropped his left shoulder and raced off to the right, Junior was ready for it. He slid in with his long legs and *CRUNCH!* He got the ball and then his little brother.

Arghhhhh!

As Darwin lay there howling in agony, Junior jumped up and showed no mercy. *2–0!*

Now, many young footballers – and especially younger brothers – would have just given up at that point, but not Darwin. No, even at that age and against an opponent who was five years older, he refused to be beaten. 'I can do this,' he told himself. He was determined to get up and go again…

This time, Darwin decided to surprise his brother by dribbling to the left, rather than the right. Then, just when it looked like he was going to try and shoot with his weaker foot, he cut the ball back with a brilliant chop that completely fooled Junior. All Darwin had to do now was pass it into the empty goal… *2–1!*

'Nice move,' Junior muttered, giving him a quick nod of respect.

The next goal felt crucial, but which brother would score it? It was Junior's turn to start with the ball and when he powered his way past Darwin's first challenge, it looked like game over. But no, *ZOOM!* Darwin raced back and threw himself down to bravely block the shot. And that wasn't all; as the ball bounced loose, he reached it first and lifted a shot over Junior's head… and in between the goalposts. *2–2!*

Wow, what a strike! There was no nod of respect from his big brother now, though; just an angry glare.

'Next goal wins!' – neither Junior nor Darwin actually said the words out loud, but they didn't have to. They both knew the score. However, just as Junior stood there planning his last move…

'Hey! Sorry we're late – come on, let's play a big game before it gets too dark!'

Noooo, what terrible timing – a large group of their friends had finally arrived. Oh well, the end of their 1-vs-1 brother battle would just have to wait until later.

As one of the oldest (and best) players there, Junior was chosen as a captain and told to pick his first teammate. So, which of his big, strong friends would he go for: Rodrigo, or Santiago, or Nico? No, he had a better idea…

'Darwin, you're with me,' Junior said with a proud smile, and his little brother beamed back at him.

Because as much as they enjoyed battling against each other, it was even more fun to play on the same team. And together, the brilliant Núñez brothers were simply unstoppable.

CHAPTER 4

SOY CELESTE!

It was the best 11th birthday present Darwin could ask for: the 2010 FIFA World Cup was going on, and Uruguay were playing in it!

'*La Celeste*' ('The Sky Blue', because of the colour of their shirts) had failed to qualify for three of the last four tournaments, but now they were back and looking better than they had since 'the glory days'.

'Did you know we won the first ever World Cup, way back in 1930?' Bibiano said as he watched Uruguay's first match together with his sons. 'And then we won it again in 1950, beating Brazil in the final–'

'Yes, Dad – WE KNOW!' Junior and Darwin said, rolling their eyes at each other. It wasn't that they

weren't proud of their country's football history; it was just that they'd heard about it hundreds of times already. From their father, but also from family friends, teachers, coaches and even random people on the streets of El Pirata. It was definitely time for Uruguay to make some *new* football history, and Darwin couldn't wait to watch it happen.

'*Soy Celeste,*

Soy Celeste,

Celeste soy yo… !' he sang along with thousands of other hopeful fans all over the country.

Winning a third World Cup trophy wasn't going to easy, though. First up, Uruguay faced France, who had finished as runners-up in 2006. Thierry Henry, Franck Ribéry, Nicolas Anelka – their team was still packed with attacking talent, even after Zinedine Zidane's retirement. So, would *La Celeste* be able to keep them quiet?

Yes! In goal, Fernando Muslera was magnificent, and so were the two Diegos at the heart of the Uruguay defence, Lugano and Godín.

'Hurraaaaaaaaay!' Darwin cried out with passion

when the final whistle blew. He had never been so excited about a 0–0 draw before.

After picking up that hard-fought first point, it was over to Uruguay's fantastic front three:

Diego Forlán, a clever, creative forward who had previously played club football for Manchester United, and now for Atlético Madrid,

Edinson Cavani, a strong, powerful striker who played for Italian club Palermo,

And Luis Suárez, an energetic and skilful striker who starred for Dutch giants Ajax.

They were each very different, but Darwin loved them all, and together, they could do it all: chase, pass, dribble, head, shoot and best of all, score. In their second game against South Africa, Forlán was Uruguay's hero with two goals, including a stunning, swerving strike from 30 yards that Darwin spent the next few days trying to copy, out on the football pitch with his friends.

'Forláááááááááááááán!'

Then against Mexico, two days before Darwin turned 11, the front three teamed up to score a terrific winning goal. It started with Forlán, who passed the ball to Cavani on the right wing, who delivered a perfect, curling cross for Suárez to score. *1–0!*

'Yessssssssssssssssss!' Darwin cheered, and he danced the whole way home, singing, '*Soy Celeste, Soy Celeste…*'

What a team! With seven points, Uruguay finished top of Group A, setting up a Round of 16 clash with South Korea two days after Darwin's 11th birthday. A win would be the perfect way to celebrate…

It didn't take long for Uruguay to take the lead. In the eighth minute, Forlán delivered a teasing cross that travelled all the way through the six-yard box to Suarez at the back post. *1–0!*

'Yesssssssssss!' Darwin cheered, jumping and down with delight.

Midway through the second half, however, his smile was turned upside down when South Korea equalised.

'Noooooooooo!' Young Darwin couldn't believe it – what was going on? Uruguay were supposed to win for his birthday! Oh well, at least their fantastic front three still had plenty of time to grab another goal…

But first Suárez got his header all wrong, and then Forlán scuffed a shot straight at the keeper.

Uh oh, the time was ticking by so quickly – there were now less than 15 minutes left!

'Come on, come on,' Darwin muttered nervously under his breath.

A Forlán corner-kick was cleared as far as Nicolás Lodeiro on the edge of the box, who nodded the ball forward to Suárez. There were teammates waiting in the middle for a cross, but no, he decided to go it alone. With a quick tap of his right foot, Suárez cut inside and curled a powerful shot past the diving South Korea keeper... and into the corner of the net. *2–1!*

'YESSSSSSSSSSSS!' Darwin screamed, punching the air with a mix of joy and relief. Phew, thanks to Suárez's moment of football magic, Uruguay *were* going to win for his birthday, after all!

La Celeste were through to the World Cup quarter-finals for the first time since 1966, and they weren't done yet. In the big game against Ghana, Uruguay were losing 1–0 at half-time, but their players refused to give up. First, Forlán equalised with another stunning, swerving strike, and then when it looked like Ghana were about to score a last-gasp winner, Suárez blocked the ball from going in... with his hands.

Penalty! Red card!

Many football fans were angry with Suárez and called him a cheat, but Darwin didn't see it that way. Perhaps it was a very Uruguayan way of thinking, but surely you had to do everything possible to help your team to win, especially in a World Cup quarter-final?

Anyway, Suárez's sending off turned out to be worth it because when Asamoah Gyan stepped up to the spot to win the game for Ghana... he hit the crossbar! The quarter-final went to extra-time and then all the way to a penalty shoot-out, where Muslera won it for Uruguay with two heroic diving saves.

After experiencing all those dramatic twists and turns, Darwin felt exhausted at the end, but nothing was going to stop him from celebrating. His country was through to the World Cup semi-finals!

'Soy Celeste...'

Now, could Uruguay beat the Netherlands and make it all the way to the final? Darwin was full of confidence as the game kicked off, but… no, with Suárez suspended, they couldn't quite do it. Despite their best, battling efforts, the Dutch attack was just too strong, and Arjen Robben scored the winning goal.

'Noooooooooo!' Darwin was very disappointed, of course, but he didn't stay down for long. Because although they hadn't won a third World Cup trophy like he'd hoped, *La Celeste* were back! Finally, Uruguay had a national team to feel proud of again, with talented players to inspire the next generation of young footballers…

'*Soy Celeste!*' Darwin sang, as dreams of the future played out in his head. Dreams where he wore the sky blue national shirt himself, and scored great World Cup goals of his own. Yes, young Darwin was determined to one day follow in the footsteps of the heroes of 2010 – Forlán, Cavani and Suárez – and become Uruguay's next superstar striker.

CHAPTER 5

ELECTRIC FOR LA LUZ

Before all that, however, Darwin had plenty of work to do and goals to score, starting with his first local team, La Luz.

After all of his practising in the playground and local fields, Darwin couldn't wait to get his proper football career started. His parents had even saved up enough money to buy him his very own pair of boots!

He proudly wore them to his first training session at La Luz, where the coach Nery Retamoso was there waiting to greet him. 'Welcome,' he said with a smile, 'Junior has already told me lots about you – all good things, I promise!'

It was supposed to be a little joke to break the ice,

but the skinny boy wearing his brother's over-sized green and white club shirt didn't laugh. Instead, he just nodded seriously and then ran off to get warmed up.

'OK then!' As Retamoso was about to find out, while the Núñez brothers shared a special football talent, their personalities were very different. Where Junior was pretty relaxed, Darwin was always raring to go; and whereas Junior was always calm and friendly, Darwin was more competitive and fiery.

'Argggggghh!' he yelled angrily every time he missed a shot, and 'ARGGGGGHH!' he yelled even louder if his team ever lost.

'Don't worry, Darwin, it's just a training match,' the coach called out, but it didn't do much good.

From day one, it was clear that La Luz had a new star player. The boy still had lots to learn, but he was lightning quick, skilful on the ball, and lethal in front of goal. In other words, he had the potential to be the perfect striker.

'Wow, he's going to be even better than his brother,' Retamoso thought to himself, as he watched Darwin score again and again. The defenders tried to chase him, push him, foul him, anything, but on the run, he was simply unstoppable! To get the best out of him, however, the coach could see that he was going to have to keep him as calm as possible.

One particularly bad day at training, Retamoso decided to send Darwin off to take a break and cool down.

'What?! NO!' his young striker argued back.

'Hey, it's just for five minutes,' Retamoso tried to tell him, but Darwin was too furious to listen. Instead, he stormed off the pitch and started walking home.

'Come on, Darwin – STOP!'

Eventually, he did, and as he turned around, Retamoso could see that all of the boy's anger had disappeared. He was back to being the Darwin that everyone loved, the nice kid who was just desperate to play football again.

'I'm sorry,' he said, giving his coach a hug. 'Are you annoyed with me?'

Instead of answering, Retamoso replied with a question of his own. 'Are you going to keep playing?'

With his head bowed down, Darwin nodded.

'Good, but you can't get so angry all the time.'

'I won't, Coach, I promise!'

Darwin was never going to be a really calm, relaxed character like his brother, but Retamoso didn't want him to be. Passion was an important part of his game, and without it, he wouldn't be the same star striker. All his coach wanted him to do was learn how to control that passion and make the most of his amazing potential.

Yes please! Darwin loved the sound of that. He was always looking for ways to improve, and so, together with his coach, he worked harder than ever on the training pitch.

When the local Artigas league kicked off, Darwin was electric for La Luz.

Passion? *Tick!*

Patience? *Tick!*

Pace? *Tick!*

Time and time again, one of his teammates played a long ball over the top and *ZOOM!* He was off, sprinting away from the defenders...

Precision? *Tick!*

... and then slamming a shot past the keeper.

Goooooooooooooooooooooooooooaaaaaaaaaaaaaaaaa aaaaaaaaaallllllllllllllllllllllllllllllllllll!!!!!!!!!!!!!!!!!

Goooooooooooooooooooooooooooaaaaaaaaaaaaaaaaa aaaaaaaaaallllllllllllllllllllllllllllllllllll!!!!!!!!!!!!!!!!!

Goooooooooooooooooooooooooooaaaaaaaaaaaaaaaaa aaaaaaaaaallllllllllllllllllllllllllllllllllll!!!!!!!!!!!!!!!!!

Progress? *Tick!*

In other words, he was well on his way to becoming the perfect striker.

'Well done, Darwin!' Retamoso cheered from the sidelines.

With his goals, assists and non-stop running, Darwin led La Luz to lots of trophies, and soon he was starring for his county, Artigas, too. In fact, he fired them all the way to a national final, but when the big day arrived, there was a big problem: he had chicken-pox!

'I'm fine, I can still play,' he tried to persuade his parents, but it was no use. He had a high fever and his whole body was covered in spots.

With their best player lying ill in bed, Artigas lost the final. *Noooooooooooo!* Darwin was devastated, but once he was feeling better, he got straight back out on the football pitch, raring to go again. Never mind, there would be lots more finals and lots more trophies ahead – Darwin was determined to make sure of that.

'One day, you're going to see me playing in Europe!' he liked to tell his coaches, and he was deadly serious about it.

From the mouths of most young footballers, those words would have sounded like arrogant fantasy, but from Darwin? No. Retamoso believed them, and he believed in his fiery young striker. The boy had so much potential that anything was possible.

CHAPTER 6

PERDOMO AND PEÑAROL

The journey from Montevideo in the south to Artigas in the north was long and boring, especially late at night, but José Perdomo didn't mind. As a football scout working for Peñarol, one of Uruguay's most famous teams, he was used to driving long distances, and besides, it was all worth it to discover the country's top young talents.

Perdomo had already made the exact same trip before, to scout and sign Junior, and now he was going back to keep the promise that he'd made at the time:

'Next year, I'll come for the skinny one.'

'*El Flaco*' was the nickname that Perdomo had used, while pointing a finger at Junior's brilliant younger brother. Even then, aged 13, Darwin had looked like a very promising player, so how much better would he look now, with another season's experience? That was the exciting question that kept Perdomo going on the dull drive to Artigas.

Once he finally arrived in the city, the Peñarol scout headed straight for the home of San Miguel de Artigas, the club where Junior used to play, and where Darwin played now, after moving up from La Luz. As he got out of his car, Perdomo could see that the San Miguel team was already warming up on the pitch in their blue and yellow shirts. Perfect timing!

Scanning the group, he spotted Darwin straight away. He was one of the tallest players in the team, with two of the longest, skinniest legs he'd ever seen. Oh and he was also the one scoring every time, and from every angle.

Control, steady, shoot – GOAL!
Control, steady, shoot – GOAL!

'He's certainly been working on his finishing,' Perdomo smiled to himself. It was a good sign to see such improvement already.

Watching the warm-up could only ever tell him a certain amount about a player, though, things like:

His pre-game attitude – *confident, focused.*

The quality of his first touch – *good.*

The power of his strike – *fierce!!*

Yes, Darwin definitely looked the real deal during the warm-up, but to answer his other, more important questions, Perdomo would have to wait to see him in action in the proper match…

Q. He was clearly tall, but could he use his height to win duels against bigger, stronger defenders?

A. Yes! Right from kick-off, Darwin battled bravely for every ball and he won a decent number of headers for such a skinny kid. But really, playing with his back to goal as a target man wasn't his style at all; as a striker, he was much better when he was racing forward at full speed…

Q. He was clearly quick, but could he use his pace in clever ways?

A. Yes! Darwin was an absolute nightmare to mark because he never stopped moving, all across the San Miguel attack, and then making sudden, explosive bursts in behind the opposition defence. As soon as a long ball was played forward, *ZOOM!* Darwin was off, sprinting away towards goal, and no-one had a chance of catching up with him…

Q. He was clearly excellent at shooting in the warm-up when the pressure was off, but could he do it when the pressure was on as well?

A. Yes! As he entered the penalty area, Darwin slowed down to steady himself and then slammed a shot past the helpless keeper.

Goooooooooooooooooooooooooooaaaaaaaaaaaaaaaaaa aaaaaaaaaallllllllllllllllllllllllllllllll!!!!!!!!!!!!!!!!!!!

As Darwin raced away to celebrate with his teammates, Perdomo felt that rush of excitement that football scouts were always searching for. A-ha, he had found a future star! Not only was the kid tall and super speedy, but he was also a hungry goal scorer. What a winning combination!

'Wow, he's perfect for European football,' Perdomo was already thinking to himself. But first things first: Darwin was perfect for Peñarol.

Usually as a scout, he had to watch a young player

four or five times before he was sure about them, but sometimes, just sometimes, one match was enough to make up his mind. For Perdomo, that was the case with Darwin that day. He knew straight away that the kid was special, so why wait around and watch him again? There was no time to waste – if he took too long, one of Peñarol's rivals might sign him up instead!

He couldn't let that happen, so as soon as the game ended, Perdomo made his move. He went over to speak to the boy's parents, whom he already knew well after scouting their other son, Junior.

'No, not Darwin too!' Silvia groaned as she watched him walking over. She knew what was coming, but what could she do? Get in the way of her son's professional football dream? No way!

Soon, they were all shaking hands to seal the deal. Yes, Darwin was going to be a Peñarol player, just like his big brother!

CHAPTER 7

FEELING FAR FROM HOME

Playing for Peñarol. As a young footballer growing up in Uruguay, what could possibly be better than that?

The club had been crowned national champions a record 49 times, and their list of famous former players was incredible:

Obdulio Varela, Uruguay's captain when they won the World Cup in 1950,

Paolo Montero, who won four Italian league titles with Juventus,

Diego Forlán and Egidio Arévalo from the Uruguay team that finished fourth at the World Cup in 2010,

Cristian Rodríguez, who had just lifted the La Liga trophy with Atlético Madrid,

Youngster Guillermo Varela, who had just signed for Manchester United…

And now, Darwin had the chance to wear the black and yellow-striped shirt and add his name to that amazing list. His dream was about to come true! At first, he was full of excitement for the football adventure that lay ahead, but as the days passed, Darwin's delight faded and the fears began to creep in. Whoa, this was really happening! His life was about to change completely – was he ready for it?

Playing for Peñarol meant leaving his family and friends in Artigas behind, and moving all the way to Montevideo to live with other kids at the club's academy. From the people, places and pitches that he had grown up with, Darwin was going to Uruguay's busy capital city, where everything would be big, scary and new. That would be a massive adjustment for anyone, but especially for a 14-year-old who had hardly even left his local area before. What if he hated it there?

'How are you feeling, son?' Bibiano asked as he helped Darwin to pack his bags for the big trip.

'OK…' he started to say, but then he decided to tell

the truth. 'Well, actually, I'm feeling a bit nervous.'

'Don't worry, you'll be fine,' his dad tried to reassure him. 'You'll have Junior nearby, and we'll try to come and visit you as often as we can. Plus, you'll be busy playing lots and lots of football!'

When his dad put it like that, it didn't sound so bad, but as Darwin boarded the bus to Montevideo on his own and waved goodbye to his parents, his fears returned and the tears streamed down his cheeks. Was this really what he wanted, or was he making a big mistake? Taking a deep breath, Darwin sat back in his seat and closed his eyes. There was only one way to find out…

'I'm doing this to achieve my dream. I'm doing this to give my family a better life.'

That's what Darwin kept telling himself during those early weeks at the academy, but it didn't make it any easier for him to adapt. The Peñarol training sessions were so intense, the other players were so talented, and they seemed to have known each other for years. Many of them were from Montevideo, and although they were all from the same country and spoke the same language, Darwin really didn't feel like he fit in. He didn't want to be 'the new kid from up north' anymore.

Back at his old clubs La Luz and San Miguel, he had been such a confident, fiery character, but now at Peñarol, Darwin hardly said a word to anyone. As hard as he tried to focus on football and impressing his new coaches, all he could think about was home: sleeping in his own bed, eating his mum's delicious cooking and best of all, going to the local field for fun kickarounds with his friends.

'So, how are you settling in?' Silvia asked him on the phone one night. She was hoping to hear her youngest son sounding happy and full of exciting stories, but instead, he burst out crying.

'Mum, I miss Artigas so much!' he sobbed.

Eventually, Silvia managed to persuade Darwin to give life at Peñarol one more go, but really, he had already made up his mind.

'So, how's it going? Are you enjoying it a bit more now?' his mum asked once he'd been there for a few more weeks.

'No, I still want to come home,' Darwin told her tearfully.

Silvia sighed. 'OK, son – don't worry, we'll book you a ticket for the bus back to Artigas, and we'll be there waiting for you.'

CHAPTER 8

SECOND TIME STRONGER

Although Darwin loved being back in Artigas, he didn't end up staying there for long. That's because Peñarol came calling again, and this time, they had a better plan to keep him there. Instead of living on his own at the academy, Darwin would live in a house where his parents could come and stay for long periods.

'How does that sound?' his agent Edgardo Laslavia asked.

'Better!' Darwin replied with a smile. Spending some time back at home had given him a chance to think about his future and what he wanted. One thing was for sure: he wasn't going to give up on his professional football dream, or his chance to play for Peñarol.

'I can do this,' Darwin told himself. Just like during his early battles against his big brother, he was determined to get up and go again. He was ready to return to the club and do things differently, developing new skills and making new friends. Yes: second time around, he would stay strong and succeed.

'Welcome back!' Fernando Curutchet, the director of the Peñarol academy, greeted Darwin as he arrived for his first training session with the Under-16s. 'Right, we've got work to do, kid.'

The idea was simple: to turn him into Uruguay's next superstar striker, 'the new Edinson Cavani'.

Yes please! Darwin loved the sound of that, and he was always looking for ways to improve. He was already tall, fast and powerful like Cavani, but to reach his hero's level, he would need to become stronger and smarter.

'Let's do this!' Darwin declared. His football passion was back and fiercer than ever.

As he got older, he naturally grew less skinny and

more muscly, but he also spent a lot of time in the gym at Peñarol, building up his body so that he could dominate defenders even more.

Strength? *Tick!* But what about the smart attacking movement? For that, Darwin studied videos of Cavani in action:

Dropping deep to collect the ball from midfield,

Reacting quickly in the six-yard box to reach a cross or a rebound,

And darting behind the defence on one of his classic diagonal runs.

'What a clever striker!' Darwin marvelled, feeling more and more inspired with each clip he watched.

And that wasn't all; Darwin was also lucky enough to see another of Uruguay's 2010 World Cup legends up close in real life. In July 2015, Peñarol made a big announcement: Diego Forlán was returning to his boyhood club for one last season!

Hurray! Darwin couldn't wait to watch him in action at the Estadio Centenario:

Somehow finding space in seemingly impossible places,

Picking out teammates with perfect passes and curling crosses,

And cutting inside off the right wing to score stunning, swerving strikes of his own.

'What a clever striker!' Darwin marvelled, feeling more and more inspired with each goal he saw. So, could he now put all those lessons from Cavani and Forlán into practice on the pitch for Peñarol?

Yes! Darwin was soon on fire for the Under-16s, causing his opponents all kinds of trouble with his speed and strength. And if there were no long-balls or through-balls for him to chase? No problem, he now had other weapons he could use too.

If passes weren't reaching him up front, Darwin just dropped deep to collect the ball, then turned and dribbled forward at full speed. *DANGER ALERT!*

And if he found that his path to the penalty area was blocked, he just used his powerful right foot to blast shots from outside the box instead. *BANG!... GOAL!*

'Well done, Darwin!' Curutchet clapped and cheered. The plan was definitely working!

Word soon spread about 'the new Cavani', and suddenly Darwin was making his way swiftly through the age groups at Peñarol. It took him a few months to adapt to Under-17s level, but once he did, he was unstoppable. In one match, he even dribbled all the way from the half-way line to score a wonder goal.

'OK, time for another new challenge,' Curutchet decided after that.

So, from the Under-17s, Darwin moved up to the Under-19s, then the Under-23s, and before he knew it, he was hearing the news that he'd been dreaming about since Perdomo first signed him for Peñarol:

'You're training with the first team today.'

Whoa, really? He was still only 16, but Darwin was about to share a pitch with heroes like Fabián Estoyanoff, Nahitan Nández and yes, Forlán himself!

So, was he nervous? Yes, of course, but as he entered the dressing room for the first time, Darwin took a deep breath and told himself, 'I can do this.'

It helped that he wasn't the only youngster amongst all the experienced Peñarol seniors. There was also midfielder Federico Valverde and winger Diego Rossi, whom he knew from the year above him at the academy. In that scary moment, it was so good to see their familiar faces.

'Hey, come sit with us,' they said, kindly making a space on the bench beside them.

Once he was changed, it was time for Darwin to go outside and show everyone what he could do. He tried his best to treat it like any other training session with the academy teams and play his usual way: with pace, power and plenty of energy and aggression. After all, this might be his only opportunity to impress the Peñarol manager, Pablo Bengoechea, so he was determined to make the most of it.

Darwin jumped for every header, raced into every challenge, chased after every pass, and took every opportunity to dribble and shoot.

He showed that he wasn't afraid to foul veteran defender Carlos Valdez, or to ignore the calls from Forlán and captain Marcelo Zalayeta to 'PASS!'

Not everything Darwin did was 100% successful, but it was the kind of confident, all-action performance that the first team players and coaches would remember for a long time.

'Well played today,' Bengoechea told him afterwards. 'I'm sure we'll see you back here again soon.'

'Yes please!' Darwin thought to himself.

CHAPTER 9

ACL AGONY

Darwin's life was now non-stop football and he loved it. He was starring for both the Peñarol Under-19s and Under-23s, *and* training with the club's first team, all at the same time. And as if that wasn't exciting enough, there was even talk of him taking the next step and making his senior debut soon!

That's because Curutchet, the academy director who had helped Darwin so much, had just been asked to take over as Peñarol's manager for the final matches of the 2016 season.

'Wow, you'll definitely get to play now,' his academy teammates joked. 'You're the coach's favourite!'

Yes, Curutchet might well give some game-time to

the club's top young talents, especially the tall striker who people were calling 'the new Cavani'… Darwin could see the path ahead, a future filled with goals and glory, and he was sprinting towards it at top speed. Unfortunately, however, it turned out to be a sad tale of too much, too fast.

Before his first-team dream could come true, Darwin was asked to appear for the Under-23s in an important match against Sud América. The Peñarol team was fighting for the league title, and their best young striker was desperate to play his part.

'OK, you can go,' Curutchet agreed reluctantly, 'but just be careful. I need you fighting fit!'

'Yes, Boss, thanks, Boss!' Darwin replied happily. There was no chance of him taking it easy, though. When it came to football, he was always all-action, no matter who the opponents were, and no matter how bad the pitch was…

During the game, Darwin jumped up for a header against a Sud América defender, but as he came back down, he landed awkwardly on the bumpy ground and his left knee buckled under the weight of his body.

'*Argghhhhhhhhhhh!*' Darwin screamed and screamed as he lay there, slapping the grass in agony. He had never felt anything like it – the pain was excruciating. Oh dear, oh dear – what had he done? He could tell from the worried look on the physio's face that it was something serious.

Eventually, Darwin was carried off the field on a stretcher and then taken straight to the hospital, where the doctor delivered the bad news:

'I'm afraid you've torn your anterior cruciate ligament,' he said, showing an X-ray of the knee.

Nooooo, not the ACL! As a fit 17-year-old, Darwin didn't know much about injuries yet, but he knew that it was pretty much the worst a sportsperson could get. He would need to have surgery, then go through lots of boring rehab. What terrible timing, just as he was about to become Uruguay's next superstar striker!

Fighting back the fear, Darwin asked the key question: 'How long will it be before I can play again?'

At first, the doctor didn't want to give him an answer, but in the end, he said, 'At least six months, but maybe more.'

GULP! That sounded like a lifetime. What on earth was Darwin going to do without football for that long?

As soon as he heard the awful news, Curutchet rushed down to the hospital to see him. 'I'm so sorry, Darwin – I knew I shouldn't have let you play today! This was supposed to be your big moment, and now... '

The manager's words trailed off because he didn't know what would happen next. No-one did. For young players like Darwin, an ACL injury could easily spell the end of their career. Even if they made a full recovery, it was still so hard for them to catch up with everyone else, after missing a whole season of football.

Curutchet believed in his young striker, though. A strong, positive mindset would be crucial for bouncing back, and Darwin definitely had that.

'Don't worry, it's just life,' he told his manager from his hospital bed. 'I will recover and keep moving forward. It's just one of those things that I have to get past.'

Slowly and sorely, the first six months went by, and then so did six more. By then, Darwin was back training with Peñarol again, but he wasn't ready to play matches yet because his knee still didn't feel right.

'Arghh, it's like there's something scraping inside!' he cried with frustration as he hobbled off the pitch.

Darwin spent hours in the gym doing special exercises to build up his body and strengthen his knee, but the nagging pain just wouldn't go away. What was causing it? Not even the doctors seemed to know.

The longer his woes went on, the more Darwin thought seriously about giving up on his football dream. Maybe it just wasn't meant to be; maybe he should just go back to Artigas, get a normal, 9 to 5 job and start again...

'No, don't quit!' Curutchet and his Peñarol teammates told him, and the club's new manager, Leonardo Ramos, said the same thing. Despite the injury problems, Darwin's incredible potential was clear to see. Pace, power, skill, determination – the kid had it all, and if he could just get fully fit again, he could still become Uruguay's next superstar striker.

Ramos was sure of that, and so he did his best to persuade Darwin to keep going. 'Remember those dreams you had when you were a young boy about playing professional football and scoring great goals in the biggest matches? Well, they can still come true, so please don't give up now!'

The support of everyone at Peñarol certainly helped Darwin to overcome his ACL agony, but it was his hero Junior, his amazing big brother, who inspired him most of all.

CHAPTER 10

JUNIOR THE HERO

For years, Junior had been a promising youth player at Peñarol too, making his way up through the ranks with the same dream as Darwin, becoming a top professional. Remember, the brilliant Núñez brothers were going to take on the football world together and become famous superstars!

But with his hopes of playing for the first team beginning to fade and his parents struggling back in Artigas, Junior had made a difficult decision that would change their family forever.

'Darwin, I'm going back to Artigas,' he announced one day.

'What, for a few weeks?' his young brother asked.

'Cool, why don't I come with you?'

'No, for good,' Junior explained. 'I'm going home to get a full-time job and earn some money to help out Mum and Dad. They need me.'

'B-but what about playing for Peñarol?' Darwin wondered, still in shock. 'This is your dream! You've been here for so long and worked so hard for this!'

His older brother sighed and shrugged. 'Look, I gave it my best shot but it wasn't quite good enough. That's all there is to it.'

'Nooooo, you can't give up yet!' Darwin wailed. 'Why don't I go instead and then you can stay-'

'NO,' Junior said firmly, putting a hand on his shoulder. 'You're staying here, bro – you have a future. You're better suited than me and you're going to be a star.'

Fighting back the tears, Darwin tried his best to argue:

'I can't let you do this. It's not fair! It should be me going home – I'm the youngest!'

But he knew his big brother, and he knew that his mind was already made up. There was nothing that

Darwin could do except thank him and promise to do everything possible to make him proud.

'I know,' Junior replied, giving him a big hug. 'I know you'll work as hard you can to achieve your football dream, and when you do, this will all be worth it.'

During all the ups and downs that followed, Darwin had never forgotten what his heroic brother had done for him:

Not when he started training with the Peñarol first team,

Not when he tore his ACL,

Not during the long months of rehab and recovery,

And not even when the niggling pain in his knee refused to go away.

Sure, there were times when he had really felt like giving up and going home, but Darwin hadn't. He had made a promise to Junior and he was determined to keep it. Yes, he was going to achieve his football dream for the both of them.

That massive moment came in November 2017, whether Darwin's knee was ready for it or not. Ramos, the Peñarol manager, decided that maybe the best way to motivate his young striker was to show him what playing professional football was really like. So for their league match away against River Plate Montevideo, he picked Darwin as one of the substitutes.

Wow, what a proud feeling it was to see his name on the squad list for the first time! And there were more nice surprises to come. With Peñarol losing 1–0 early in the second half, Ramos turned to his bench and fixed his eyes on his young striker.

'Darwin, go and get warmed up,' he shouted.

'Who, me?' was his first thought. Whoa, was he really about to make his first team debut?

Yes! In the 63rd minute, Darwin ran on to replace Argentinian attacker Maxi Rodríguez, wearing the Number 26 on the back of his shirt. This was it; the day he, and Junior, had always dreamed of. So, could he make an instant impact as a super sub?

No, sadly not. In fact, within seconds of his arrival on the pitch, River Plate Montevideo scored again! Darwin could only watch from the halfway line as Facundo Boné volleyed the ball in at the back post. *2–0!*

'Oh well,' Darwin thought to himself, 'at least we've still got 30 minutes left to turn things around… '

When the game kicked off again, he threw himself straight into the action. A one-two in the box with captain Cristian Rodríguez didn't quite work out, but Darwin kept going and kept causing problems for his opponents.

'Hey, watch out for the 26 – he's faster than he looks, and fiercer too!'

Bursting with passion and energy, Darwin showed that he wasn't afraid of anyone or anything. When Cristian pulled one goal back from the penalty spot, he was the first Peñarol player to rush in and grab the ball off the keeper.

'Let's goooooooooo!' Darwin yelled out as he ran back for the restart. Now, could he score a second goal to tie the game for his team?

With time ticking away, a cross from the left flew just over Lucas Viatri's head, but there was Darwin, racing in right behind him. He chested the ball down brilliantly and then fired off a shot with his left foot… *SAVED!*

Chance wasted? No, Darwin did well to slide in and steal the ball back, but his second shot was saved too.

'Nooooooo!' he groaned at the sky, but he kept going and kept causing problems.

When a pass flew over Darwin's head and rolled towards the corner flag, he chased after it and managed to keep the ball in play. OK, what next? Skill time! One on one with the River Plate right-back, Darwin faked to go left, then right, and then with a burst of pace, he dribbled to the left, skipping past his opponent on the outside. He was into the box now, where he laid the ball back for Cristian to strike… *BLOCKED!*

This time, the rebound fell to Gastón Rodríguez, who blasted a shot just over the crossbar. *So close!*

When the final whistle blew a few seconds later, Darwin let out a big sigh of disappointment. His Peñarol debut had ended in defeat! But while he always hated losing, at least he could walk off the pitch knowing that he had done everything possible to impress his manager, and to make his brother proud.

'Well done, Darwin – what a performance, you

were electric out there!' Junior praised him afterwards. 'But next time, try to score a goal, yeah? That's what strikers are for!'

CHAPTER 11

BOUNCING BACK AGAIN

The great news was that Darwin had just achieved his dream of playing professional football for his favourite childhood club.

But the really bad news? His knee *still* didn't feel right! In fact, in the days after his debut, he could hardly walk, let alone run. Darwin didn't want to just keep playing through the pain; to become a superstar striker, he needed to feel fully fit and firing! Something was clearly wrong, so the Peñarol doctors decided to do more medical tests, and at last, they discovered the problem: an extra bit of bone was growing on his kneecap and causing all the discomfort.

'A-ha, so I was right – there *was* something scraping

inside!' Darwin said. It was a relief to finally know what the issue was, but to fix it, he was going to need to have more surgery, this time in Argentina, and then spend more months away from the football pitch.

Again, the timing was terrible, just as he was breaking into the first team, but he was determined to stay strong and positive. He had bounced back from a long injury once; he could do it again. He had to; for his brother, his parents, and for himself.

Slowly and sorely, the first six months of 2018 went by, but this time, when Darwin started training again in June, his knee felt so much better. No scraping feeling, no niggling pain – he was healed at last! Now, it was time to get fully fit and firing…

At Peñarol practice, Darwin worked harder and harder until he was back to his electric best, bursting past any defenders that tried to get in his way.

ZOOM!… BANG!… GOAL!

'Whoa, our rivals better watch out,' his teammate Fabián Estoyanoff said with a smile. 'The new Cavani is coming for them!'

Peñarol's new manager, Diego López, was delighted

with his striker's progress, and so when the new Uruguayan league season kicked off in July, he put Darwin straight into the starting line-up. Hurray, it felt like he was about to make his first-team debut all over again!

Playing at home against Racing Club de Montevideo, Peñarol took the lead in the very first minute, but sadly it wasn't Darwin who got the goal. It was his strike partner, Gabriel Fernández, who was in the right place at the right time to head in from Fabián's perfect cross. *1–0!*

Never mind, the main thing was that the team was winning. Now, could Darwin get his name on the scoresheet too?

'Yesss, pass it!' he called out for the ball, in space in the six-yard box, but Agustín Canobbio decided to shoot instead, and a defender blocked it.

Later in the first half, Darwin used his strength to hold off the centre-back, and then spun and shot, but the keeper saved it.

Midway through the second half, an even better chance arrived. Racing into the area to reach Maxi's through-ball, Darwin steadied himself and then struck the ball with power towards the bottom corner, but it flew wide of the far post.

'Arghhhhhh!' Darwin screamed, swiping at the air in frustration. It was a golden chance wasted to win the game for Peñarol; maybe he wasn't quite back to his best just yet...

After 84 minutes of passion and energy, Darwin's comeback match came to an end. As he walked slowly around the edge of the pitch and over to the bench, he felt exhausted but so excited to be back.

'Well played,' his manager told him. 'Now, you need to rest.'

After such a serious injury, it was important for Darwin to take things slowly. So, in the next few matches, he didn't play at all, and after that, López just used him as a second-half super sub. The plan was that he would come on and terrorise the tired defenders with his explosive pace...

'Yes, Coach!' Against Boston River, Darwin got the ball wide on the right wing and burst his way into the box, dancing past one tackle and then another. *Olé!*

What a run! Now, for the finish. The angle was too tight for the shot, so Darwin decided to set up Gabriel instead. His cross was flying straight towards his strike partner's head, but no, the goalkeeper managed to flick it away with his finger-tips.

Nearly!

Against CA Atenas de San Carlos, Darwin made a brilliant late sprint into the box, just as Agustín curled in a cross from the left. He followed the ball all the way, and stretched out his long right leg, but he just couldn't quite reach it before the defender.

Unlucky!

Darwin felt like he was getting closer and closer to scoring his first senior goal, but when would it finally come?

The answer was 13th October 2018, at home against CA Fénix. Darwin was back in the Peñarol starting line-up by then, playing on the left side of the attack. He was working hard and playing well, but there was still one major thing missing…

As soon as he saw Gabriel pass the ball out to Fabián on the right wing, *ZOOM!* Darwin was off, bursting into the middle and in between the Fénix defenders. Now, he just needed a good cross, and that's exactly what his teammate delivered, sliding the ball straight to him on the edge of the six-yard box. Surely, he couldn't miss? No, with a calm flick of his right foot, Darwin guided it into the net. *1–0!*

Goooooooooooooooooooooooooooaaaaaaaaaaaaaaaaa aaaaaaaaaalllllllllllllllllllllllllllllllllllllll!!!!!!!!!!!!!!!!!!

Yessssss, his big moment had arrived at last – he was off the mark in professional football! As he raced over to the corner flag, Darwin kissed the Peñarol badge on his shirt and then jumped up high to punch the air. What a proud feeling it was to be living his childhood dream!

'Well done, Darwin!' his teammates cheered. 'You definitely deserve that!'

Peñarol finished the season in first place, but they still had a final decider to play against their greatest rivals, Nacional. If they won, Peñarol would lift their 50th league title; if they lost, Nacional would lift their 47th.

'Come onnnnnnnn!' Cristian cried out as he led

the Peñarol team out onto the pitch at the Estadio Centenario. Darwin was a little disappointed to only be on the bench for the big game, but he was hoping to still help his team as a super sub.

Early in the second half, it was Nacional who took the lead, but instead of bringing on Darwin and his energy, López went for the experience of Maxi and Fabián. And it worked, because from a Fabián free-kick, Fabricio Formiliano headed in an equaliser to take the game to extra-time.

'Come on, Coach – bring me on, bring me on,' Darwin muttered under his breath, as his legs grew more and more restless on the bench. But no, López decided to stick with the same team for extra-time, and six minutes later, Peñarol were ahead, thanks to a penalty from Cristian.

'Yessssss!' Darwin shouted, jumping out of his seat. Now, they just had to hold for another 24 minutes, and the trophy would be theirs.

With his team focused on defending, he wasn't expecting to get any game-time, but in the 115th minute, Gabriel got injured, and so Darwin finally came on. So, could he make an instant impact and seal the victory for Peñarol? No, when his one chance arrived, he scuffed his shot straight at the keeper. *Arghhh!* Never mind, that miss was soon forgotten because they had a league title to celebrate!

'YESSSSSS!' Darwin roared with pride as he ran around the field, hugging each and every teammate. 'We did it, we did it!'

Campeones, Campeones, Olé! Olé! Olé!

A winner's medal, a trophy, and a massive Peñarol party – what a perfect way for Darwin to end his difficult, bounce-back year!

CHAPTER 12

URUGUAY'S NEXT STAR STRIKER?

At the age of 19, Darwin was still far from the finished superstar, but his exciting potential was now clear for everyone to see: his teammates and his opponents; his club and his country.

Fabián Coito, the coach of the Uruguay Under-20s, had no doubt that Darwin was the striker his team needed for the upcoming 2019 South American Championships in Chile. The squad was already packed with skilful wingers and little playmakers:

Nicolás Schiappacasse,

Emiliano Gómez,

Juan Manuel Boselli

Agustín Dávila...

But where was Uruguay's big guy up front, who would make life difficult for defenders and bang in lots of goals? Well, now they had Darwin to do that! Sure, he had only scored one in 14 games so far for Peñarol, but Coito had full faith in him.

'Just you wait and see – he's going to be our next star striker!' the coach declared confidently.

When Uruguay lost 1–0 to Peru in their opening game, however, people had their doubts about that.

'Yes, he's fast and powerful, but the kid can't finish! He had two easy chances in the last five minutes – how on earth did he miss BOTH of them?'

But did Coito listen to the critics and drop him to the bench for their next game against Ecuador? No, he stuck with his striker, and Darwin helped secure a 3–1 victory with a clever, chipped assist for Nicolás.

'OK, that was a great pass, but where are the GOALS?!'

Unfortunately, as hard as he tried, Darwin just couldn't hit the net at the South American Championships. 6 games, 0 goals – and when Coito did eventually drop him to the bench for a few matches, Uruguay won them all, even beating Brazil! The good news was that they had qualified for the FIFA Under-20 World Cup later that year, but would Darwin even make the squad?

Oh yes, Coito wasn't going to give up on him that easily! When Uruguay took to the pitch in Poland for their first group game against Norway, Darwin was still there, wearing the Number 9 shirt and leading the line as the central striker. Phew! So, with the whole football world watching, could he put on a better performance for his country this tournament?

Norway's national teams were famously solid in defence, and this one also had a highly-rated goalscorer in attack: a fast, powerful forward called Erling Haaland. Oooooooooh, it was a battle of the new young big guys – who would come out on top?

Haaland was the first to score, but his header was ruled out for offside. Now, what could his rival striker do at the other end?

As Ronald Araujo launched a long ball from defence, *ZOOM!* Darwin was off, bursting between the Norway centre-backs to get there first. Winning the race was impressive, but what he did next was even better. On the edge of the box, Darwin calmly chested the ball down, let it bounce once, and then whipped a swerving shot over the keeper's head and into the net. *1–0!*

Goooooooooooooooooooooooooooaaaaaaaaaaaaaaaaa aaaaaaaaaalllllllllllllllllllllllllllllllll!!!!!!!!!!!!!!!!!

Whoa, what a stunning strike! 'Come onnnnnn!' Darwin screamed as he slid across the grass on his knees. Soon, he was at the bottom of a huge pile of players, including all of the substitutes.

Buzzing from that wonder goal, Uruguay were soon on the attack again. From the left wing, Brian Rodríguez dribbled all the way into the box at speed and set up midfielder Francisco Ginella to score. *2–0!*

Midway through the second half, Darwin should have scored again, but one-on-one with the keeper, he somehow blasted his shot wide.

'Noooooooo!' he groaned with both hands on his head, and a confused look on his face. What had just happened?

Never mind, luckily that miss was soon forgotten

because Brian grabbed a late third goal to seal
the win. *3–1!*

Uruguay were off to a flying start, and their good
form continued. First, they beat Honduras 2–0, and
then they did the same to New Zealand, with their
star striker scoring again.

After a one-two with Martin Barrios, Emiliano
Ancheta sprinted into space on the right wing and
then fizzed the ball across the six-yard box, looking for
his striker. The cross was perfect and so was Darwin's
movement, pulling away into the gap between the
New Zealand defenders. And the strike? A calm,
first-time finish that flew past the keeper in a flash.

*Goooooooooooooooooooooooooooaaaaaaaaaaaaaaaaa
aaaaaaaaaalllllllllllllllllllllllllllllllllllll!!!!!!!!!!!!!!!!!!*

'Yesssssssss!' Darwin cheered, shaking both fists
in the air. He always loved scoring proper striker's
goals like that.

With three wins out of three, Uruguay were
through to the World Cup Round of 16, where they
met Ecuador, the reigning South American champions.

'Come on, we beat these guys twice in Chile, and

now we're going to beat them again!' their captain
Bruno Méndez declared before kick-off, and it all
started so well for Uruguay. Brian almost scored in the
fifth minute, and six minutes later, Ronald succeeded,
bundling the ball in after a goalmouth scramble. *1–0!*

Unfortunately, Uruguay couldn't hold on to
their lead, though, and by half-time, Ecuador were
level. With the game so finely balanced, the next
goal felt more important than ever. So, which team
would it go to?

In the 65th minute, Darwin had a golden chance to
be Uruguay's hero. As he chased after a hopeful long
ball, the Ecuador defender made a complete mess of
his clearance, kicking it backwards into Darwin's path.
What an opportunity! But as he slid in, he poked a
weak shot too close to the keeper. *SAVED!*

'Nooooooo!' Darwin groaned, lying flat on
the grass.

This time, his miss really did matter. Instead, it
was Ecuador who scored the next goal, and the one
after that too, with Bruno giving away a penalty and
receiving a red card. Sadly that was game over, and

World Cup over, for Uruguay.

As he looked back on the long journey home, Darwin felt disappointed, but not distraught. Although his team hadn't got as far as he'd hoped, there were still plenty of positives to take from the experience. Despite a few major misses:

He had played well in every game,

He had scored two goals – one good and one great,

And he had learned a lot from battling against the world's best young defenders.

No, Darwin wasn't the finished superstar yet, but could he go on to become Uruguay's next star striker one day in the future? Sure, why not?! With his potential, and lots more hard work, anything was possible.

CHAPTER 13

SETTING OFF FOR SPAIN

Darwin returned to Peñarol in time for the start of
the Torneo Intermedio, the middle part of the league
season. Perfect!

'This is going to be *my* tournament,' Darwin told
himself determinedly. He was aiming to build on his
World Cup experience and break out as his club's
brightest new star.

In recent years, Peñarol had developed a great
reputation as a home of top young talent, and scouts
from all over the world were paying close attention to
every player coming up from the academy.

Jonathan Rodríguez had been signed by Portuguese
giants Benfica,

Nahitan Nández by Boca Juniors from Argentina,

Diego Rossi by Los Angeles FC from the USA,

Santiago Bueno by Barcelona,

And Federico Valverde by the mighty Real Madrid!

So, could Darwin be next to make the exciting move to another country, maybe even to Europe? As much as he loved playing for Peñarol, that had always been his ultimate dream, but he knew that he wasn't the club's only promising young attacker. There was also his Uruguay Under-20 teammate Brian, plus the two Facundos, Pellistri and Torres.

The other three, however, were all small, skilful wingers, whereas Darwin offered something totally different. A tall striker with explosive pace and power – he was exactly what all the top teams were looking for. But now it was time to really stand out on the pitch for Peñarol.

In their first game, at home against Boston River, Darwin was picked to start alongside Brian in attack.

'Let's do this!' they cheered together before kick-off.

Brian scored the first goal in the 10th minute, but after that, it was all about Darwin.

From inside his own penalty area, Walter Gargano launched a hopeful long ball forward, and *ZOOM!* Darwin was off, racing away from the defenders to reach it first. Part one: complete – now, could he keep calm and score?

Yes! As he entered the box, he slowed down, looked up at the target, and then blasted a powerful shot past the keeper. *2–0!*

Goooooooooooooooooooooooooooaaaaaaaaaaaaaaaaaa aaaaaaaaaallllllllllllllllllllllllllllllllllllllll!!!!!!!!!!!!!!!!!

Darwin was so delighted with his finish that he jumped over the advertising boards and kissed the club badge right in front of the Peñarol fans.

And there were more celebrations ahead in the second half. First, Brian dribbled forward and slipped the ball through to Darwin, who curled a composed, first-time shot into bottom corner. *3–0!*

'Thanks for the pass!' he called out, pointing at Brian, as they ran towards each other for a hug and a high-five.

After scoring only one goal in his first 14 games for Peñarol, Darwin had just added two more in the last

50 minutes! Now, what about another to complete the hat-trick?

Yes please! He was hungry for more, and determined to take his chances. When a good pass from Guzmán Pereira arrived at his feet, Darwin burst between two defenders with a clever first touch and then *BANG!* slid an unstoppable shot past the keeper. *4–0!*

Goooooooooooooooooooooooooaaaaaaaaaaaaaaaaaa aaaaaaaaaalllllllllllllllllllllllllllllllllll!!!!!!!!!!!!!!!!!!!

Hurray, hat-trick hero! As he raced over to the corner flag, Darwin pulled a funny face for the fans and then punched the air again and again. What a proud feeling it was to be Peñarol's star striker!

But the big question now was: how much longer would he stay there? Two goals for his country at the Under-20 World Cup, and then a hat-trick in his first game back for his club – Darwin was really starting to catch the eye. Would the scouts keep watching and waiting until the end of the Uruguayan season in December, or would any European clubs come calling during the summer?

Unión Deportiva Almería, a football team in
the south of Spain, had been stuck in the Second
Division for several years, but under new owner Turki
Al-Sheikh, a businessman from Saudi Arabia, they
were desperate to get promoted back to La Liga. To
succeed, they were going on a mega summer spending
spree. They had already brought in:

Defenders Jonathan, Nikola Maraš, and Iván Balliu,

Midfielders Radosav Petrović, Valentín Vada,
and Ante Ćorić

And attackers José Lazo, Juan Muñoz, and
Arvin Appiah.

There was still one crucial piece of the perfect
promotion team missing, however: a star striker.
Almería's previous top scorer, Álvaro Giménez, had
just been signed by Birmingham City, so they needed
someone new. Someone young, someone exciting,
someone with explosive pace and power who could
fire the team all the way to Spain's top division.

Hmmmm, how about… Darwin? Well, his
goalscoring record so far wasn't brilliant, but he
certainly ticked all of the other boxes! After watching

him in action, the club's manager, Pedro Emanuel, decided to make an offer.

'Almería? Come on, you can do better than that! What's the rush? Stay until the end of the season, and I bet you'll have all the biggest clubs chasing you.'

Those were the thoughts of his agent and the Peñarol Director of Football, but Darwin didn't see it that way. He knew that he still had work to do to reach his full potential, and Almería sounded like the perfect place for him to keep developing, away from the pressure of Europe's top leagues.

Plus, there was one other very important factor for Darwin: his family. If he signed for Almería, he would earn enough money to finally pay his brother back, look after his parents properly and buy them that new home he had always promised, in an area that would never flood. What if he never got this life-changing chance again?

'It's very kind of you to think of us, but you have to do this for *YOU*,' Silvia kept telling her son, but Darwin's mind was already made up. One day, he would return to his favourite club and wear the black and yellow shirt again, but for now, his future lay at Almería.

'I want to go,' he begged Peñarol. 'Please let me leave.'

By late August 2019, the deal was done. A transfer fee had been agreed, a five-year contract had been signed, and a big plot of land had been bought in Artigas for building the new Núñez family home. Waving goodbye to his home country and his boyhood club, Darwin set off for Spain and exciting times in Europe.

CHAPTER 14

BETTER AND BETTER AT ALMERÍA

'I'm very excited to be here at a big club,' Darwin told the journalists as he smiled for the cameras wearing the red and white stripes of Almería. The supporters were excited too, but in the end, they had to wait over a month to see their new record signing in action.

Why? Well, after sitting on the subs bench for the first game of the season against SD Huesca, Darwin picked up a minor injury in training, and so the coaches decided to give him some time to adapt to his new team in a new league in a new country. The kid was still only 20, after all! In Spain, he would be battling against better, stronger defenders and the pitches they played on were watered regularly, which made the passing slicker and the game faster.

'Don't worry, he'll soon get up to speed,' David Badia, Almería's assistant manager, assured Emanuel. 'He's a really hard worker and he's one of the quickest strikers I've ever seen!'

Darwin wasn't worried either. No, from the moment he arrived in Almería, he knew that he had made the right decision. The city wasn't big, loud and bustling like Montevideo; it was smaller and quieter, a lot more like Artigas, the area where he'd grown up. The local people were friendly and spoke the same language as him, but he could still walk around without being asked for autographs all the time. Yes, when the time came, this was going to be the perfect place to take his first steps in European football.

At last, in early October, Darwin was ready for Spanish league action, but sadly, he didn't get the dream debut he was hoping for. When he came on as a half-time sub against Sporting Gijón, Almería were already 4–1 down, and there was nothing he could do to save the day.

Oh dear, what a disastrous start to life in Europe,

but luckily there was good news to lift Darwin's spirits: he had been called up to the Uruguay senior squad!

Yes, with Suárez and Cavani both out injured, the national team manager Óscar Tabárez was looking to the future. In the two friendlies against Peru, Brian started up front with Maxi Gómez, but in the second, with Uruguay losing 1–0, Tabárez turned to his bench and called for… Darwin!

Hurray! He was bursting with pride as he ran on to the field, and desperate to make an instant impact. As Matías Viña curled a cross into the box, Darwin made a late dash to the front post and threw himself forward for a diving header. *BOOM!* From down on the grass, he turned and watched as the ball landed in the bottom corner. *1–1!*

Goooooooooooooooooooooooooaaaaaaaaaaaaaaaaaa aaaaaaaaaallllllllllllllllllllllllllllllllllllll!!!!!!!!!!!!!!!!!

Whoa, now this really was the dream debut he was hoping for – five minutes after coming on, and Darwin was already celebrating his first international goal! Uruguay's next star striker was here to save the day…

'Vamooooooooos!' he yelled as he raced towards the

corner flag, with his new teammates trailing behind.

Still buzzing from that magical moment, Darwin returned to Spain feeling more determined than ever. Now that he had scored for his country, it was time to do the same for his club.

Darwin's first goal for Almería was a penalty against Extremadura in late October, and that gave him the confidence boost he really needed. Over the next few weeks, he scored a few more –

A header against Real Zaragoza,

A tap-in against Mirandés,

– and by December, Darwin was on fire, terrorising the better, stronger defenders of the second division.

When Juan played a pass through, *ZOOM!* Darwin was off, bursting between the Lugo centre-backs. Then with his first touch, he guided the ball into the net with the side of his right foot.

Goooooooooooooooooooooooooooaaaaaaaaaaaaaaaaa aaaaaaaaaalllllllllllllllllllllllllllllllll!!!!!!!!!!!!!!!!!!

Pace, power and a calm shot to finish – it was the kind of goal he had scored so many times before back in Uruguay for La Luz, San Miguel and Peñarol, and now at last Darwin was doing the same in Spain.

'That's it – keep going!' Guti, the former Real Madrid star and new Almería manager clapped and cheered, and Darwin soon had a second goal to celebrate.

As the season went on, his confidence grew and he just got better and better. The Real Oviedo centre-back thought he had all the time in the world to play the ball back to his keeper, but no, *ZOOM!* Almería's amazing Number 21 raced in to reach it first. Then he calmly dribbled around the keeper and passed it into an empty net. Easy!

With two more strikes against Deportivo de La Coruña in early March, Darwin moved onto 12 goals in his last 18 games. Wow, he was in the best scoring form of his life! Surely he was going to fire Almería all the way to La Liga?

But no. Just as the supporters began to get excited, the COVID-19 pandemic spread around the world and the football season had to be suspended.

Oh no, what now? As Spain entered lockdown, Darwin decided to fly back to Uruguay to be with his family, but he didn't relax and take a break. Instead, he carried on working hard at home: looking after his body, eating a healthy diet, and practising his skills on his own on the local pitches. Then when it was allowed, he even hired a personal trainer to help him get stronger and faster than ever.

'Bro, you're like Cristiano Ronaldo these days!' Junior joked. 'A total fitness freak!'

It was all worth it, though, because when the Spanish league finally returned three months later, Darwin was back with a BANG…

Goooooooooooooooooooooooooooaaaaaaaaaaaaaaaaaa aaaaaaaaaallllllllllllllllllllllllllllllllllllllll!!!!!!!!!!!!!!!!!

He scored the winner against Albacete and another key goal against Rayo Vallecano to finish the season in fourth place in the race for the Golden Boot. Unfortunately, Almería finished the season in fourth place too, which meant no automatic promotion but a play-off spot instead.

'OK this it, guys,' another new manager, José Gomes, told them before the semi-final against Girona. 'Our second chance to get the job done. This time, we *have* to take it.'

But after a 1–0 defeat in the away leg, they then went 1–0 down at home as well. Oh dear, the pressure was really on the Almería players now, and their star striker in particular.

'Let's go Darwin, we need a goal!' the fans cried out.

As hard as he tried to help his team, he couldn't quite grab a goal himself. He did, however, set one up with a brilliant bursting run. Dropping deep to collect the ball, Darwin turned and dribbled forward at full speed, leaving his opponents trailing behind. Then when he reached the edge of the box, he fooled the defenders with a sudden cutback and slid the ball across for José to score instead.

'Come on, we can still win this!' Darwin urged his teammates on as they raced back for the restart.

But no, it was Girona who scored the next goal, and that was it – game over, season over. Almería would be staying in the second division for another year.

Noooooooooooooooo!

As he walked off the pitch, Darwin felt so disappointed. Their mission had been promotion to

La Liga, and despite all their hard work, they had failed. The big question now was: would he be staying at Almería?

CHAPTER 15

BENFICA'S RECORD BUY

After a slow start at Almería, Darwin had adapted well to Spanish football and finished his first season with 16 goals in 32 games. Those were good numbers for such a young striker, and there were clear signs that he would keep getting better and better. That's why so many scouts all across Europe were paying close attention. There was interest from:

Brighton and Southampton in the English Premier League,

Wolfsburg and RB Leipzig in Germany's Bundesliga,

Inter Milan and Napoli in Italy's Serie A,

Benfica in Portugal's Primeira Liga,

And Darwin was even recommended to Spanish

giants Barcelona by one of his Uruguay heroes.

'You should take a look at Núñez at Almería,' Luis Suárez suggested to his club. 'He's a special talent, and I know a thing or two about strikers!'

Barcelona did send scouts to watch Darwin play, but in the end, they decided that he was too young and inexperienced at the top level, and so they signed another forward, Francisco Trincão, instead.

Oh well, Barcelona's loss was Benfica's gain. Yes, in the end, it was the Portuguese club with its proud history that won the race to sign Darwin for a record fee of €24million.

'Wow, that's a lot of money to pay for a kid playing in the Spanish second division!' many people thought, including some of Benfica's own fans, but the manager Jorge Jesus had no doubts about Darwin. On top of his pace and power, the Uruguayan was also humble and hard-working.

'I know I still have a lot to learn,' he had told the coaches when he first arrived at the club, 'and I'm ready to listen.'

With a positive attitude like that, Darwin was sure

to succeed. He was going to be Benfica's new superstar striker, and help lead them to the league title again. The previous season, they had finished as runners-up behind their big rivals Porto, but not this year; not after their summer spending spree…

Benfica kicked off the 2020–21 season away at FC Famalicão with an all-new and expensive attack:

Everton, a winger from Brazil,

Luca Waldschmidt, a forward from Germany,

And wearing the Number 9 shirt, Darwin!

So, could they form a successful partnership straight away? Oh yes! Luca scored Benfica's first goal, after a clever flick-on from Darwin, and Everton scored the second a few minutes later. In the second half, Darwin set up Luca again with a perfect cross to complete a wonderful 5–1 win.

Whoa, Benfica's new front three were off to a flying start! And the good times continued:

Darwin set up the second goal against Moreirense,

The winner against SC Farense,

And then another goal for Luca against Rio Ave.

Four games, four wins, and five assists already for

Benfica's new Number 9! Darwin was always happy to help his teammates, but as a striker, he was also desperate to score a goal of his own, his first for his new club…

After a disappointing defeat in Champions League qualifying, Benfica had dropped down into the Europa League, where they began with a trip to Poland to take on Lech Poznan. It wasn't quite as exciting as facing Real Madrid or Manchester United, but Darwin didn't mind. He couldn't wait to test himself in one of Europe's biggest club competitions.

As half-time approached, Benfica were drawing 1–1, but when Gilberto delivered a cross from the right, up jumped Darwin in the middle, high above his marker, to power an unstoppable header past the Lech keeper.

Gooooooooooooooooooooooooooaaaaaaaaaaaaaaaaaa aaaaaaaaaalllllllllllllllllllllllllllllllllllll!!!!!!!!!!!!!!!!!!

At last, his first for Benfica! 'Vamoooooos!' Darwin roared with passion, making a heart shape with his hands for all fans watching at home on TV. Now that he had scored one, he was hungry for more…

As the pass arrived from Everton, Darwin had his

back to goal, but not for long. After a touch to the left, he suddenly spun and cut the ball back to the right, sending it through the legs of the defender. *Nutmeg!*

Now for the finish – Darwin calmly curled the ball around the keeper and into the bottom corner.

Goooooooooooooooooooooooooooaaaaaaaaaaaaaaaaaa aaaaaaaaaalllllllllllllllllllllllllllllllllllllll!!!!!!!!!!!!!!!!!

Darwin slid towards the corner flag on his knees, with the biggest smile on his face. What a game he was having, but how about one more goal to complete the hat-trick?

In the last minute of the match, Rafa Silva chipped a dangerous ball across the six-yard box and there was Darwin, racing away from his marker to head in at the back post.

Goooooooooooooooooooooooooooaaaaaaaaaaaaaaaaaa aaaaaaaaaalllllllllllllllllllllllllllllllllllllll!!!!!!!!!!!!!!!!!

Yesssssssss, hat-trick hero – after going five games without a goal, Darwin had just scored three in the last 50 minutes!

And four days later, he followed that up with his first goal in the Primeira Liga against Belenenses.

This time, it was Luca setting up his strike partner with a lovely through-ball. *ZOOM!* Darwin timed his run to perfection and then calmly dribbled around the last defender and the keeper, before firing into the empty net.

Goooooooooooooooooooooooooooaaaaaaaaaaaaaaaaa aaaaaaaaaalllllllllllllllllllllllllllllllllll!!!!!!!!!!!!!!!!!!!!

'Yesssssss!' Darwin yelled, punching the air with both fists. That was more like it – a proper striker's goal! He could feel the confidence flowing through his body and all the way down to his shooting boots.

After those four goals in five days, Europe's biggest clubs were now watching Darwin closely. According to the newspapers, Italian giants Juventus were preparing to make a huge offer in January, and so were Barcelona, who had already changed their mind about signing him.

But no, Benfica's new superstar striker wasn't going anywhere... yet.

'Darwin will remain at the club until at least 2022,' the president quickly announced. What was the hurry? The boy was still only 21 years old, and getting better and better with every game!

'He will learn with me,' his manager, Jesus, told the journalists. 'Darwin was Benfica's most expensive purchase, and when there is no pandemic, he will be the most expensive sale. He will be a world-class player.'

FIRST-SEASON FRUSTRATIONS

Darwin was off to a brilliant start at Benfica, but there were difficult times ahead. Just when he was beginning to feel unstoppable, he fell ill with a cough, a high fever, and aches all over his body. Uh-oh, he could guess what it was before he even took a test: COVID-19.

'Noooo, not now!' he groaned to himself.

In the end, Darwin only missed a few weeks of football, but it took him a lot longer to get back to top form and top speed. At first, the goals continued to flow –

Another neat finish against Lech Poznan in the Europa League,

A tap-in against Portimonense in the Primeira Liga,
– but as the season went on and the games got
bigger, he began to struggle badly.

Against their title rivals Porto, Darwin had two
massive chances to win the match for Benfica, but he
missed them both and it finished 1–1.

Nooooooooo!

Against Nacional, he was subbed off after 60
minutes, and in the local derby against Sporting
Lisbon, he really looked like a player who was lacking
confidence and form. There were none of his usual
explosive bursts of speed, no thumping shots, no
heroic, leaping headers. Darwin hardly touched the
ball at all up front, and when he did, his control was
poor and his passing was all over the place. After 78
minutes, he was subbed off again, and Sporting went
on to win 1–0.

Boooooooo!

Benfica were slipping down the table – from 1st
to 2nd, to 3rd, to 4th – and Darwin was in danger
of slipping out of the starting line-up. In the
Primeira Liga, his record now stood at three goals

in 15 games, and the supporters were losing their patience with him.

'*A world-class player? Rubbish! He's the worst striker we've ever had!*'

'*What a waste of space and money! Why on earth is he playing ahead of Haris Seferovic and Gonçalo Ramos?*'

Darwin tried his best to keep going and just ignore the negative comments, but it wasn't easy. In the end, after talking to a sports psychologist, he decided to delete his social media account for a while. That way, he could stay focused on football and bouncing back from the bad spell he was going through.

'I can do this,' Darwin told himself with the same determination as ever.

A goal against Famalicão gave him a much-needed boost, but a few games later against Farense, Darwin was taken off early in the second half and left the field in tears. Argggh, it was so frustrating, after such a strong start to his first season at Benfica!

Poor Darwin, what was going on? Well, the main problem was that he was playing through pain. Yes, unfortunately, he was injured again. As well as a hamstring tear, he also had another niggling, long-term knee issue, this time with his other leg.

Darwin would probably need to have more surgery to fix the problem, but he wanted to wait and play on until the end of the season if possible to help his team. The only way he could do that, though, was to play a lot less football, so from March until the end of the league season in May, Darwin moved to the bench and became Benfica's second-half super sub instead.

GOAL! He scored a late tap-in against Paços Ferreira.

GOAL! Against Portimonense, he showed a flash of his famous pace and power as he burst between the centre-backs and fired past the keeper.

'Vamoooooos!' Darwin roared with delight, and so did his captain Pizzi as he jumped into his open arms.

ASSIST! Against Nacional, Darwin set up two goals for Gonçalo with dangerously quick counter-attacks.

ASSIST! And on the final day against Vitória Guimarães, he picked out Haris with a perfect cross from the left wing.

'Yesssssssss!' Darwin yelled out, shaking his fists in the air and letting all his frustration out.

His first season at Benfica had been full of ups and downs, so he was pleased and proud to finish off with 14 goals and 12 assists. Those numbers weren't bad at all, considering his illness and injuries, and Darwin was confident that he could – and would – do a lot better next season once he was fully fit again after surgery.

Sadly, the long, slow recovery meant that he would have to miss out on that summer's Copa América with Uruguay, but Darwin knew that it would be worth it in the end. Because once he was back to top form and top speed again, he was ready to take the next step and become a consistent, world-class superstar striker, for his club and for his country.

SECOND SEASON SUPERSTAR

The Benfica doctors were expecting Darwin to be out for at least four months, but instead he came racing back after three, looking better than ever.

'Whoa, take it easy!' The club doctors tried to slow him down, but Darwin was a man on a mission. He had work to do and goals to score. The 2021–22 season had already started, and Benfica needed their superstar striker back in action.

'I'm ready!' he kept telling his manager until eventually he gave in.

Jesus let Darwin play the last 20 minutes against Gil Vicente, and then the first 60 against Tondela. There were no goals, but there were also no niggling knee

pains anymore. Right, that was enough of a warm-up; it was time to hit top speed and top form again…

Away at Santa Clara, Everton received the ball on the halfway line, and *ZOOM!* Darwin was off, sprinting in between the defenders and into the space where he expected the pass to go. When he got there, he dribbled into the box and calmly lifted a shot over the diving keeper.

Gooooooooooooooooooooooooooaaaaaaaaaaaaaaaaaa aaaaaaaaaalllllllllllllllllllllllllllllllllllllll!!!!!!!!!!!!!!!!!!

It was a classic Darwin run and finish – hurray, Benfica had their star striker back! And scoring his first goal of the season wasn't the only thing that he was celebrating. Tucking the ball under his shirt, Darwin sucked his thumb in front of the cameras, which was football language for: we're having a baby!

Yes, his partner, Lorena, was pregnant; he was about to become a father! So, would his life-changing news make any difference to the way Darwin played? Yes, it made him even more determined to succeed. 10 minutes after his first goal, he scored again, this time with his left foot, and that was only just the start of a remarkable run...

Two against Boavista,

One against Braga,

Three against Belenenses,

And then three more against Famalicão!

That was two hat-tricks in three Primeira Liga games for Darwin, and he almost made it three in four a week later against Marítimo, but the keeper made some top saves and Jesus took him off with 15 minutes to go.

'Ohhhhhhhh!' The fact that Darwin was disappointed about only scoring two goals in a game showed just how far he'd come in the last few months. He was really thinking like a superstar striker now, as well as acting like one. He was up to 13 league goals for the season already, which was more than double his previous total, and it was still only December!

Wearing his curly hair down to his shoulders, Darwin now looked like his hero Cavani, and he was playing like him too: the powerful runs, the clever link-up play, the leaping headers and the high-quality finishes.

Plus, there was also some of his other national hero Suárez in the way Darwin played: the endless energy, the non-stop chasing and the never-give-up fighting spirit.

What a winning mix it was! But what were the main reasons behind Darwin's sudden fantastic form? Well:

He was fully fit again after his first-season injury frustrations.

He had found his perfect position: starting on the left side of Benfica's front three, but with the freedom to burst into the middle.

He had formed an amazing understanding with his fellow attackers: Rafa, Everton, Gonçalo, Pizzi, João Mário, Roman Yaremchuk, Alejandro Grimaldo… with so many talented teammates around him, he always had chances to score!

He was full of confidence: on the ball, on the run, in the air and most importantly, in front of goal. Darwin wasn't just hitting and hoping anymore; he was now expecting to score every time.

And in most matches, he succeeded:

One against Tondela,

Another two against Santa Clara,

Two against Vitória Guimarães,

And then another three against Belenenses!

Wow, with his third hat-trick of the season, Darwin had now scored 24 goals in just 24 games. That made him the most lethal striker in any of Europe's top leagues!

At home in the Primeira Liga, there was only one question left for Darwin to answer: could he become a big-game player for Benfica? So far, he had still not scored a single goal against Porto or Sporting. Could he change that record in the second Lisbon Derby of the season, away at the Estádio José Alvalade?

In the opening minutes, Sporting came so close to scoring, but somehow their striker Paulinho missed a golden chance. *Phew!* Now, could Darwin do any better at the other end for Benfica? *Yes!*

When Jan Vertonghen launched a long pass forward, *ZOOM!* Darwin was off, racing away from the Sporting centre-backs to reach it first. As the ball bounced, he had a defender closing in behind him, and the goalkeeper rushing out towards him, but with a beautiful flick of his right boot, Darwin lifted the ball over his upstretched arms and into the net. *1–0!*

Goooooooooooooooooooooooooooaaaaaaaaaaaaaaaaaa aaaaaaaaaalllllllllllllllllllllllllllllllllll!!!!!!!!!!!!!!!!!

Yesssssss, Darwin had done it; he had scored in the Lisbon Derby! With his arms out wide, he raced towards the corner flag and then slid across the grass on his knees. What a feeling!

Benfica hadn't won the game yet, though. Darwin still had more lots more work to do, and he never stopped running:

Dropping deep to hold the ball up for his teammates,

Bursting forward to try and score a second goal,

And rushing in to put the Sporting defenders under pressure.

Then, in the final minute, Darwin led Benfica up the pitch on one last counter-attack. From the halfway line, he dribbled the ball all the way to the Sporting box, where he set up Gil Dias to seal the victory. *2–0!*

What a win for Benfica, and a man-of-the-match

performance from their Number 9! With a goal and an assist, there was no doubt that Darwin was the Lisbon Derby hero!

Soon he was the Primeira Liga top scorer as well, finishing with a total of 26 in just 29 games. But Darwin knew that it wasn't all about the number of goals; it was also about the quality and the impact of them. Scoring a hat-trick in a 7–1 win was great, but what about helping his team to win tighter, more important matches?

Darwin had shown he could do that too. During his superstar second season, he had proved that he was a big-game player: in the Portuguese league, and most of all, in the UEFA Champions League.

CHAPTER 18

CATCHING THE EYE IN THE UCL

Yes, this time, Benfica had made it through to the Champions League group stage, and Darwin was so excited to test himself in Europe's greatest club competition. He had grown up watching the big games on TV in Uruguay, and now he was actually going to be playing in them – unbelievable!

When he saw the other teams in Benfica's group, however, Darwin's excitement was mixed with fear: Barcelona, Bayern Munich and Dynamo Kyiv.

Oof, talk about a Group of Death! But while it was definitely going to be tough, this was the dream that Darwin had been working towards: competing at the top level against the best teams in the world.

'Bring it on!' he told his Benfica teammates.

After a 0–0 draw away in Kyiv, it was time for Barcelona to visit the Estádio da Luz. Although the glory days of Suárez, Lionel Messi and Neymar Jr were now over, they still had plenty of other world-class players all over the pitch:

Memphis Depay in attack,

Frenkie de Jong and Sergio Busquets in midfield,

And in defence, Gerard Piqué and Darwin's international teammate Ronald Araujo.

It was good to see his fellow countryman, but once the game kicked off, they were opponents, not friends.

Vamoooooooos!

In the biggest match of his career so far, it only took Darwin two minutes to make an impact. As soon as Julian Weigl won the ball back in midfield, he knew exactly what to do. *PING!*

ZOOM! Darwin was after it in a flash, bursting past the Barcelona defenders, but by the time he reached the ball, he was wide on the left wing. OK, what now? With no teammate waiting in the middle for the cross, Darwin decided to dribble into the box himself. After a couple of stepovers, he cut inside past Eric Garcia and then *BANG!* He went for the shot. Barcelona were expecting him to aim for the far corner, but instead, he surprised Marc-André ter Stegen and beat him at his near post. *1–0!*

Gooooooooooooooooooooooooooaaaaaaaaaaaaaaaaaa aaaaaaaaaalllllllllllllllllllllllllllllllllllll!!!!!!!!!!!!!!!!!!

'VAMOOOOOOOOOOS!' Darwin roared as he slid across the grass on his knees. What a magical moment – he had just scored his first Champions League goal against the mighty Barcelona!

And Darwin wasn't done there. He almost scored again early in the second half, but his long-range shot bounced off the post. So close! Oh well, never mind, there were would be more opportunities ahead. When Benfica won a late penalty, he stepped up and coolly sent ter Stegen the wrong way. *3–0!*

With his tongue out and a huge smile on his face, Darwin jumped up and punched the air. Mission accomplished! He was catching the eye already in the Champions League.

And soon Barcelona weren't the only big team that

Darwin had scored against. He grabbed a late goal away against Bayern Munich in a 5–2 defeat, and then another much more important late goal away against Ajax in the Last 16.

After a 2–2 draw at home, Benfica travelled to Amsterdam with a simple plan: defend well and try to nick a winning goal. That sounded achievable, but with Ajax dominating the game, how on earth were they supposed to score? Darwin spent most of the match battling in vain for the ball and making runs in behind, where the pass never came. He never gave up, though, and in the 77th minute, at last a golden chance arrived. Alejandro's free-kick was swinging straight towards him on the edge of the six-yard box...

This was it; he simply had to score. Using his strength to hold off his marker, Darwin waited for the perfect moment and then *LEAP!* Up he jumped to meet the ball first with a powerful flick header that flew into the net. *1–0!*

Gooooooooooooooooooooooooooaaaaaaaaaaaaaaaaaa aaaaaaaaaallllllllllllllllllllllllllllllllllll!!!!!!!!!!!!!!!!!

Yesssssss, Darwin had done it again – when his

team needed a hero, he had come up with another big goal in a big game. At the age of 21, he was already playing like an experienced Champions League striker, and thanks to him, Benfica were heading through to the quarter-finals for the first time since 2016!

There, they faced another famous European club with a long and successful history: Liverpool. Jürgen Klopp's side had already lifted the trophy in 2019, and now they were looking to do it again. But could Benfica be the team to stop them? Darwin was ready to do his very best.

In the first leg at the Estádio da Luz, Liverpool were 2–0 up and cruising by half-time, but early in the second half, the home side came fighting back. As Rafa raced forward up the right, Darwin made a clever move in the middle, drifting away from Virgil van Dijk and over to the other centre-back, Ibrahima Konaté…

As the cross came in, Konaté made a total mess of his clearance, and Darwin was right behind him to pounce on the mistake, like any superstar striker should. A touch to control and then *BANG!*…

*Gooooooooooooooooooooooooooaaaaaaaaaaaaaaaaa
aaaaaaaaaalllllllllllllllllllllllllllllllllllll!!!!!!!!!!!!!!!!!!*

Thanks to Darwin, Benfica were back in the game!
Grabbing the ball out of the net, he ran back for
the restart.

Unfortunately, the first leg finished 3–1 to Liverpool,
but Darwin and his teammates arrived at Anfield
feeling confident that they could turn things around.
Why not? They had one of the world's most in-form
players up front!

Sadly, it wasn't to be for Benfica, but Darwin did
still get on the scoresheet again, eventually. His first
goal of the night was disallowed, and his vicious volley
was brilliantly saved by Alisson, but the Uruguayan
never gave up. Late on, he raced into the penalty area
unmarked, and lifted the ball past the Liverpool keeper
with a smart finish.

'Offside!' the linesperson ruled, but no, luckily for
Darwin, VAR disagreed.

*Gooooooooooooooooooooooooooaaaaaaaaaaaaaaaaa
aaaaaaaaaalllllllllllllllllllllllllllllllllllll!!!!!!!!!!!!!!!!!!*

His sixth in his first season in the Champions

League. By then, it was too little too late to save the day for Benfica, but still, Klopp was very impressed. And not just by Darwin's goals, but by his all-round, all-action performances.

'Wow, well played,' the Liverpool manager said when he went over to speak to the striker after the final whistle. 'You're an absolute nightmare to play against!'

It turned out to be the first of many conversations between the two of them.

CHAPTER 19

A PREMIER LEAGUE PLAYER!

As the 2022 summer transfer window opened, there was one item at the top of almost every team's shopping list: a new striker. Yes, Europe's biggest clubs were all looking to sign guaranteed goalscorers, and they were willing to spend lots of money to get them. So, who were the best young forwards out there?

Well, there was Harry Kane at Tottenham,

Kylian Mbappé at PSG,

Erling Haaland at Borussia Dortmund…

And Darwin at Benfica!

Yes, after his superstar second season, he was now one of the most highly-rated young attackers in the world. And when Kane and Mbappé both decided to stay at their clubs for another year, Darwin's value shot up even higher. Suddenly 'Haaland' and 'Núñez' were the two names everyone was talking about, but where would they end up?

Darwin was attracting interest from Real Madrid, PSG, Bayern Munich and Inter Milan, plus all of the biggest clubs in England:

Manchester United already had Cavani, but they wanted to replace him with 'the new Cavani',

Manchester City were still looking for the right replacement for Sergio Agüero,

Arsenal were making a fresh start without Pierre-Emerick Aubameyang and Alexandre Lacazette,

And Liverpool were starting to move on from their fantastic front three of Sadio Mané, Roberto Firmino and Mo Salah.

Let the battle begin! At the start of the summer, Darwin and his agent spent a long time speaking to lots of different clubs and lots of different managers. They each had exciting plans to win lots of trophies, but which team's style would suit him the best? From the very beginning, Darwin's heart said…

'Liverpool'.

Having played against them in the Champions League, he could see exactly how he would fit into their front three, using his pace and power on the counter-attack.

Plus, Darwin loved everything about Liverpool.

Big club? *Tick!*

Amazing stadium and supporters? *Tick!*

Great manager? *Tick!*

Great players? *Tick!*

Champions League football? *Tick!*

The chance to win lots of trophies? *TICK!*

Yes, Liverpool felt like the perfect place for Darwin, but before he made his final decision, he asked for some advice from a Uruguay teammate who had spent four years at the club.

'You'll love it there,' Suárez assured him, 'and the fans will love you too!'

OK, Darwin's mind was made up; Liverpool was definitely where he wanted to go. But the next question was: would Benfica let him leave?

The Portuguese club were desperate to keep their

star striker, of course, but after some difficult years during the COVID-19 pandemic, Liverpool's offer was one they simply couldn't refuse.

'Making a sale of €75 million plus €25 million in add-ons is not open to discussion,' the Benfica president Rui Costa told the fans as they reluctantly agreed the deal.

And so on 13th June 2022, the big news was announced to the world: Darwin was now a Liverpool player, and a Premier League player too!

'Dreams do come true,' he posted on social media under a picture of him proudly wearing the famous red shirt and sitting next to the famous club badge.

It was a moment and a feeling that Darwin would never forget, but he didn't have long to enjoy it. Soon, it was time for him to focus on football again; to meet his new teammates and get ready for the new season. As Liverpool's new record signing, the pressure was really on to succeed.

Vamooooooooooos! Darwin couldn't wait. Mané, Divock Origi and Takumi Minamino had all moved on to new clubs, which meant that Liverpool now had five attackers fighting for three starting spots:

Salah,

Firmino,

Diogo Jota,

Luis Díaz,

And Darwin.

'Let the battle begin!' he thought to himself. After his experiences at Almería and Benfica, Darwin knew that it would take time to adapt to a new league in a new country, but he was confident that he could do it again.

In pre-season, Darwin scored four goals against RB Leipzig, then two more against AC Milan, and he carried on that strong form in Liverpool's first competitive match of the season: the FA Community Shield against Manchester City.

There would be mouthwatering duels going on all over the pitch, but the one that most people were talking about was between the big guys up front: Darwin vs Erling Haaland, City's new €60 million signing. So, which pacy, powerful young striker would win this time?

The answer was… Darwin! Even though he only came on in the 60th minute, he changed the game completely.

After sliding a pass across to Mo, he turned and sprinted forward into the space between the City centre-backs. Mo's cross was perfect, and as Darwin headed the ball goalwards, it flicked off a defender's arm.

'Handball!' he screamed, racing over to the referee. Craig Pawson waved play on, but after a VAR check, the penalty was eventually awarded. Mo stepped up and… scored. *2–1 to Liverpool!*

'Come onnnnnnnn!' Darwin roared as they celebrated in front of the fans. Suárez was right; they loved him already!

And by the time the final whistle blew, the Liverpool supporters loved their new striker even more. In the last minute, Mo chipped a cross to Andy Robertson at the back post, who nodded it down for Darwin to score with a diving header. *3–1!*

Goooooooooooooooooooooooooooaaaaaaaaaaaaaaaaaa aaaaaaaaaalllllllllllllllllllllllllllllllllllllll!!!!!!!!!!!!!!!!!!

First he had won a penalty and now he had scored as well – what a dream debut! Darwin was so excited that he took his shirt off and waved it in the air. A yellow card? He didn't care about that; he was Liverpool's new hero!

One game, one goal, one trophy – Darwin was off to the perfect start and the Premier League season was about to kick off.

CHAPTER 20

HIGHS, LOWS AND LOTS MORE TO COME

In their opening league match, it was Liverpool's super sub to the rescue again. With his team 1–0 down, Darwin came on early in the second half and caused all kinds of problems for the Fulham defence.

As Mo raced forward on the right, Darwin sprinted through the middle and into the box. Then, with an extra late burst of speed, he got himself in front of Tosin Adarabioyo, just as the cross came in…

The ball was flying towards him at speed, but Darwin still had the confidence and skill to flick it between his legs and into the back of the net. *1–1!*

Goooooooooooooooooooooooooooaaaaaaaaaaaaaaaaaa aaaaaaaaaalllllllllllllllllllllllllllllllllllll!!!!!!!!!!!!!!!!!!!

After a quick high-five with Mo, Darwin stood in front of the fans and punched the air with passion. What an instant impact! One on his Liverpool debut, and now one of his Premier League debut too – he was looking like a goal machine already!

15 minutes later, Darwin returned the favour by setting up Mo to score the second goal. Two games, two goals and two assists – surely Klopp couldn't keep him on the bench any longer?

No, for their next game against Crystal Palace, the Liverpool manager moved Darwin into the starting line-up. So, with a whole 90 minutes to play, how many goals could he score and how much chaos could he create? Sadly, the result this time was zero goals and too much chaos.

'You've got to keep calm,' Klopp was always telling him, but urged on by the amazing Anfield atmosphere, Darwin felt anything but calm.

First, he skied a volley from inside the six-yard box,

And then from a similar position, he sliced a shot that bounced back off the post.

Arghhhhh! With each miss, Darwin got more and

more frustrated, until Joachim Andersen took full advantage. A push and a few angry words from the Crystal Palace defender was all it took to push Darwin over the edge. He turned and threw his head into Anderson's face, right in front of the referee. Uh oh…

Red card! Nooooo, what a disaster! Darwin had been sent off on his Anfield debut. After the highs of scoring against Manchester City and Fulham, this was the lowest of the lows.

'Look, those kind of things are going to happen every game in England,' Suárez told his fellow Uruguayan on the phone. 'Defenders will keep trying to wind you up, so you've got to stay strong and ignore it. Don't worry, you'll be fine – just don't do that again!'

The next day, Darwin posted an apology to everyone at Liverpool. 'I'm here to learn from my mistakes and it won't happen again,' he wrote. 'I'll be back.'

But when he returned from suspension, Darwin found it hard to rediscover his top scoring form. There were still lots of good moments:

A great sliding strike against Arsenal,

A match-winning header against West Ham,

Two fantastic finishes against Southampton,

His first Champions League goals for Liverpool against Rangers, then Ajax, then Napoli.

But there were also lots of not so good moments –

A disappointing game in the Merseyside Derby against Everton,

Two one-on-ones with the keeper wasted in a 2–1 loss to Leeds United,

An open-goal howler against Ajax,

Missed chances against Rangers, then Manchester City, then Tottenham.

When the club season stopped in mid-November, Darwin's record stood at nine goals in 18 games. He wasn't yet banging them in like he had at Benfica, but it wasn't too bad, especially considering Liverpool's struggles. In the Premier League, they were down in seventh place, already 14 points behind the leaders Arsenal.

Oh well, perhaps a change of scene and a change of focus might help. The 2022 FIFA World Cup was about to begin in Qatar, and Darwin couldn't wait to play a key part for Uruguay. 12 years on from the magic of 2010, he was really hoping to make his nation proud again. With Suárez and Cavani now coming to the end of their international careers, it was the perfect time for the country's next star striker to step forward and shine.

Vamoooooooooos!

Uruguay had been placed in one of the tournament's toughest groups, along with South Korea, Ghana and Cristiano Ronaldo's Portugal.

Darwin, however, was feeling excited rather than worried. To win the World Cup, Uruguay were going to have to beat the big teams anyway, so bring it on!

For their opening match against South Korea, he started alongside Luis Suárez and his old Peñarol teammates Facundo Pellistri and Fede Valverde in attack. On paper, it looked like a very exciting line-up, but on the pitch, somehow things just didn't quite click.

A moment midway through the second half seemed to sum it all up. With a sudden burst of speed, Darwin raced away from his marker and up the left wing.

'Cross it!' Luis shouted, pointing to where he wanted the ball to go, but Darwin waited too long and ended up passing it straight to the South Korea keeper. At the back post, Luis turned away in frustration, and eventually the match ended 0–0.

Never mind, at least Uruguay still had two more group games to go. Could they perform better against Portugal? This time, Edinson was picked as Darwin's partner, but despite lots of running, neither of them could make any impact and they were both subbed off after 70 minutes.

'Noooooo, this is not how my first World Cup was supposed to go!' Darwin groaned to himself as he slumped down in his seat.

The 2–0 defeat was a huge disappointment, but it wasn't tournament over just yet for Uruguay. If they beat Ghana and Portugal beat South Korea, then they could still reach the Round of 16...

For the big game, Luis was back alongside Darwin in attack, and together with winger Giorgian de Arrascaeta, they got off to a flying start.

Darwin crossed the ball to Luis, but his shot was

saved, and Giorgian nodded in the rebound. *1–0!*

Then six minutes later, Darwin headed it down to Luis, who lifted it over to Giorgian, who volleyed a shot past the keeper. *2–0!*

Hurray, that was more like it from Uruguay's amazing attackers! So, job done? No, unfortunately there was bad news in the other group game. Against the odds, South Korea had fought back from 1–0 down to beat Portugal 2–1 with a goal in the 91st minute! It meant that if they didn't score again in the dying seconds, Uruguay were heading home...

By then, Darwin had already been taken off, so all he could do was urge his teammates on from the sidelines. 'Vamoooooooooooooooos!'

'Penalty!' cried Edinson, but the referee shook his head.

Maxi Gómez's shot was heading for the bottom corner, but the Ghana keeper dived down and saved it.

Moments later the final whistle blew, and it was all over. Uruguay had been knocked out in the World Cup group stage... on goal difference.

NOOOOOOOOO! As the sad truth sunk in, Luis

cried, Edinson argued and Darwin walked slowly around the pitch with his head in his hands. Three games, zero goals – he really felt like he'd failed and let his whole nation down.

'We didn't deserve this ending but the dream ended,' he posted on social media. 'Sorry to all the Uruguayan people.'

There was no time for Darwin to dwell on his World Cup disappointment, though; he headed straight back to Liverpool to try and help lift them up the Premier League table. That was the plan anyway, but despite his best efforts, his bad scoring form continued.

In the League Cup, Darwin ran and ran, causing lots of problems for the Manchester City defenders, but could he find the net? On three occasions, he got into the perfect position, but with the pressure on, he dragged his shot wide, and Liverpool lost 3–2.

Nooooooo!

Four days later, The Reds bounced back to beat Aston Villa in the Premier League, but for Darwin, it was another frustrating game in front of goal.

When Ezri Konsa miskicked the ball high into the

air and towards his own goal, Darwin knew that he wouldn't get a better chance to score. *ZOOM!* He chased after it and as the ball dropped down on the edge of the box, he watched it carefully onto his favoured right boot. So far so good, but when it came to the shot, Darwin hit it straight at the keeper. *Saved!*

Nooooooo!

What? How? Why? His strike partner Mo couldn't believe it, and neither could his manager on the touchline. How many more incredible chances was Darwin going to waste? The answer was: A LOT. He missed another two one-on-ones against Aston Villa, and then two more against Leicester City.

NOOOOOO!

Oh dear, it was all going wrong for Darwin. The fans of other football teams were starting to laugh at his finishing, and the Liverpool fans were losing faith in him too. Yes, he worked hard and made great runs, but he was supposed to be a striker, and he couldn't even score with an open goal!

Klopp, however, refused to give up on his record signing. Despite all the bad misses, he kept believing in Darwin and kept helping him to get better.

'Stay calm!'

'Keep moving and making those runs!'

'Come on, I can do this,' Darwin kept telling himself. With his manager's support, he was determined to come back stronger, just like he had at all of his previous clubs: Peñarol, Almería and best of all, at Benfica.

'I don't think I'm playing well at the moment,' he admitted honestly, 'but I always want to improve.'

In the FA Cup against Wolves, Darwin finally ended his difficult run. This time, when Trent Alexander-Arnold delivered a brilliant cross to the back post, he did as his manager said and stayed calm. With the side of his left foot, Darwin guided the ball into the bottom corner.

Gooooooooooooooooooooooooooaaaaaaaaaaaaaaaaaa aaaaaaaaaalllllllllllllllllllllllllllllllllll!!!!!!!!!!!!!!!!!

At last! As he raced away to celebrate, Darwin stuck out his tongue and pointed at his head again and again, as if to say, 'See, I'm focused and ready to shine!'

So, would that be the first of many great goals? Not straight away. Darwin did score a stunning flick against Real Madrid in the Champions League and then two more against Manchester United in the Premier League, but with Liverpool fighting hard for fifth place, he found himself in and out of the starting line-up in the last months of the season.

Despite that, Darwin still finished with 15 goals from 42 games. Those were decent numbers for his first year in English football, and there would be more to come next season. Darwin was confident about that, and so was his manager.

'A lot more, that's for sure,' Klopp declared. 'The potential is incredible. Speed. Attitude. A real worker. It is really exciting.'

CHAPTER 21

LIVERPOOL'S NEW NUMBER NINE

During the summer, Chelsea made a cheeky attempt to sign Darwin, and Atlético Madrid asked about a loan swap with João Félix, but fortunately Liverpool said no to both ideas.

Phew! Darwin didn't want to go anywhere else; he was desperate to stay at the club and do whatever it took to become their superstar striker. His second season would be a second chance, and just like at Benfica, he was ready to make the most of it. He even had an exciting new shirt number to prove it.

'I'm really happy to wear Number 9,' Darwin announced ahead of the new season, 'and very proud too. Previously other players represented this number really well, and now it is my turn to wear it.'

Yes, he was following in a long line of legends:

Billy Liddell,

Ian St John,

Ian Rush,

Robbie Fowler,

Fernando Torres,

And most recently, the Brazilian Roberto Firmino.

It was a shirt that would only add to the pressure that Darwin was playing under, but he was determined to stay calm and succeed. First task: fire his way back into the Liverpool starting line-up.

Vamoooooooooos!

The Reds kicked off the new Premier League season with a front three of Mo, Luis Díaz and Diogo Jota. Oh well, Darwin would just have to sit on the bench for now, waiting impatiently to become Liverpool's super sub...

In the opening match against Chelsea, he came on and made an instant impact, but sadly his last-minute strike swerved just wide of the post. So close to the winning goal!

A week later against Bournemouth, the game was already won by the time he entered the field. No chance!

When Klopp brought Darwin on in Liverpool's next match against Newcastle, however, the situation was very different. Not only was his team 1–0 down, but they were also down to 10 players, after Virgil van Dijk had received an early red card. So, from that bad position, could Darwin come on and change the game, with only 15 minutes to go? Challenge accepted!

As Trent played the ball forward to launch the next Liverpool attack, Darwin moved across the frontline, ready and waiting to burst in behind the tired Newcastle defence with his tremendous pace and power. Diogo's pass looked like it would be blocked by Sven Botman, but no, the defender could only flick the ball behind him, towards his own goal. *ZOOM!* Darwin was on to it in a flash and racing into the box...

This was it; the kind of chance that a superstar striker simply HAD to take. 'Just stay calm and concentrate,' Darwin told himself, slowing down to get his shot just right. *BANG!* He aimed low and hard for the far bottom corner and hit his target with perfect accuracy. *1–1!*

Goooooooooooooooooooooooooooaaaaaaaaaaaaaaaaaa aaaaaaaaaalllllllllllllllllllllllllllllllllllll!!!!!!!!!!!!!!!!!

Yesssssssss, what a finish! With a whoop of delight, Darwin raced over to the corner flag and slid on his knees in front of the fans. Hurray, he was off the mark for the season, and there were still over 10 minutes of the match to go. Could he now go on and win it for Liverpool?

Deep in injury time, Mo got the ball just inside the Newcastle half, and *ZOOM!* Darwin was off again, racing in behind the defence.

Could Mo pick him out with a perfect pass? Yes!

And could Darwin score with a perfect shot? Yes! After taking a moment to steady himself, he fired the ball into the far corner of the net again. *2–1 to Liverpool!*

Goooooooooooooooooooooooooooaaaaaaaaaaaaaaaaaa aaaaaaaaaalllllllllllllllllllllllllllllllllllll!!!!!!!!!!!!!!!!!

'Vamooooooooooos!' Darwin roared with passion.

Two goals in 12 minutes to win the game for his team – what a super sub!

After that, surely Klopp couldn't keep Liverpool's new Number Nine on the bench any longer? No, Darwin had successfully fired his way back into the starting line-up, and this time, he was going to make sure that he was there to stay.

Against Aston Villa, he set up Mo with a clever flick header. *ASSIST!*

Then against West Ham, he raced on to Alexis Mac Allister's chipped pass and scored with a sublime volley. *GOAL!*

'Mate, that was magic!' Mo cheered as Darwin made a heart shape with his hands and held it up for the Liverpool fans, who were going wild all around him at Anfield.

Núñez! Núñez! Núñez!

Suddenly, the confidence was flowing through his body again, and Darwin was making a real difference for his club in every match he played. Yes, there were still a few spectacular misses, but he was finding the net a lot more often now.

He scored from the penalty spot in the Europa
League against LASK,

Then tapped in with his left foot in the Premier
League against Nottingham Forest.

He curled a shot into the top corner against
Bournemouth,

Then another into the bottom corner
against Burnley.

'Darwin is in a really good moment,' his manager
Klopp praised him at a press conference. 'He is in the
middle of the team and everyone is really happy with
him, I am very happy with him.'

Thanks, Boss! Yes, not only had Darwin improved
his finishing, but he had also improved his link-up
play with his fellow Liverpool attackers. He was now
everywhere on the pitch, and involved in everything.
He set up more goals for Mo against Brighton, Everton
and Brentford, plus others for Luis, Curtis Jones,
Dominik Szoboszlai and Cody Gakpo.

'Thanks, Darwin!'

With two more brilliant finishes in a 4–0 away win
at Bournemouth in January, he became the first player

in the whole of the Premier League to reach 10 goals and 10 assists in all competitions that season.

As well as shining for his club, Darwin was shining for his country. Under new manager Marcelo Bielsa, he was now Uruguay's number one superstar striker, and he was finally following in the footsteps of Forlán, Suárez and Cavani, by scoring goal after goal:

A late equaliser against Colombia,

A header to beat Brazil,

A quick counter-attack to beat Argentina,

Then two more goals to beat Bolivia…

'Vamooooooooooooos!'

Darwin was very proud of all the progress he had made. For Uruguay, he had put his 2022 World Cup failure behind him and was now leading them forward, towards the tournament in 2026.

And for Liverpool, he had battled on through his early struggles in England, always listening and always learning, and now he was exactly where he wanted to be. He was flying high, and so was his team.

'Núñez again!' cried the commentator on TV. 'The Reds are really on a roll!'

Yes, with Darwin, Mo and Diogo on fire together up front, Liverpool were sitting top of the Premier League table, two points ahead of their big rivals Manchester City. Could The Reds go all the way and lift the title again?

CHAPTER 22

THE QUEST FOR THE QUADRUPLE

Just days after Darwin's double against Bournemouth, everyone at Liverpool Football Club was left stunned by some massive news: their manager had decided to leave at the end of the season!

'I love absolutely everything about this club, I love everything about the city, I love everything about our supporters, I love the team, I love the staff. I love everything,' Klopp wrote. 'But I know that I cannot do the job again and again and again and again.'

Noooooooooo, don't goooooo! At first, Darwin and his teammates were shocked and devastated, but as the news sunk in, those feelings soon switched to focus and determination. Yes, together they were going to give their amazing manager the best goodbye by winning as many trophies as possible!

Vamooooooooooos!

Could Liverpool really win the Quadruple? Why not?! There was only one way to find out...

1) The League Cup?

With important assists against West Ham in the quarters and Fulham in the semis, Darwin helped Liverpool to reach the final at Wembley. When the big game against Chelsea arrived, however, unfortunately he wasn't fit enough to play his part. A muscle injury meant that he had to cheer his team on from the stands instead, but he wasn't going to let that stop him from celebrating.

'If we score, I'm running onto the pitch!' Darwin warned everyone sitting around him. They thought he was joking, but no, he was serious, and he kept his promise. When Virgil headed in the winner late in extra time, Darwin leapt out of his seat, pushed past the other players in his row, ran down the steps, jumped over two barriers, and then raced out onto the grass, punching the air with passion.

Pain, what pain? They had done it; Darwin was about to lift his first major trophy for Liverpool! It was another of his football dreams come true, and when the celebrations began, he was at the centre of everything, the only grey tracksuit in a sea of red shirts, singing and smiling.

Campeones, Campeones, Olé! Olé! Olé!

Liverpool! Liverpool! Liverpool!

Right, one trophy won; three to go…

2) The FA Cup?

Liverpool cruised through the early rounds of the tournament, but in the quarter-finals, they faced their big rivals Manchester United, away at Old Trafford. Big games didn't get much bigger than that, and Darwin was back from injury just in time. Hurray!

After 10 minutes, Liverpool were already losing 1–0, but they didn't let their heads drop. Instead, they kept attacking and attacking, until eventually the equaliser arrived. Just before half-time, Darwin reacted brilliantly in the box and slid the ball across for Alexis to score. *1–1!*

Game on! Moments later, Liverpool were ahead.

Darwin's curling strike was saved, but Mo was there to smash in the rebound. *2–1!*

Yessssss, comeback complete! From there, they should have gone on to win the game comfortably, but the Liverpool forwards failed to take their chances, and in the end, Manchester United made them pay.

2–2,

3–2 to Liverpool,

3–3,

4–3 to Manchester United!

Noooooooooooo! What? How? When the final whistle blew, Darwin stood there staring up at the sky in disbelief. Despite dominating the game, somehow Liverpool had just been knocked out of the FA Cup!

Oh well, at least they still had two more trophies to fight for...

3) The Europa League?

Liverpool were the favourites to win the Europa League and they showed why by thrashing Sparta Prague 5–1 and then 6–1 in the Last 16.

In the first leg in Prague, Darwin was Liverpool's main man. First, he cut inside off the left wing and curled in a swerving shot from outside the box.

Goooooooooooooooooooooooooooaaaaaaaaaaaaaaaaa aaaaaaaaaallllllllllllllllllllllllllllllllllllll!!!!!!!!!!!!!!!!!

Then, 20 minutes later, Darwin raced on to Alexis' pass and calmly fired the ball into the far corner.

Goooooooooooooooooooooooooooaaaaaaaaaaaaaaaaa aaaaaaaaaallllllllllllllllllllllllllllllllllllll!!!!!!!!!!!!!!!!!

The movement, the finish – he made it all look so easy! Darwin jogged away with his arms out wide and then jumped up and karate-kicked the corner flag. Why? Because he had just scored his 16th goal of the season, taking him past his previous year's total already! And there were still three months of matches left to play, including a Europa League quarter-final against Atalanta…

Everyone expected Liverpool to win, especially at home at Anfield, but instead, the Italians raced away to a shock 3–0 victory.

Whoa, what on earth was going on?! After playing so well together all season, suddenly the Liverpool team looked so tired, slow and sloppy. The defenders were making big mistakes, and their attackers were missing crucial chances. Cody, Diogo, Luis and Mo all wasted good opportunities too, but it was Darwin who wasted the most and the best of them.

One on one with the Atalanta keeper, he snatched at his shot and poked the ball well wide.

When he was played through again, Darwin's first touch took him too wide and his shot was easily saved.

And finally, after collecting a great pass from Cody, he scooped his shot over the bar.

'Noooooo, you've got to keep calm and take your time there!' Darwin moaned at himself. Arghhh, it was like the previous season all over again!

Liverpool did bounce back to win the away leg 1–0, but it wasn't enough, and they were knocked out of the Europa League, again at the quarter-final stage. Oh dear, from fighting for another three trophies, they were now down to just one. After such a strong start, their season was in danger of falling apart…

4) The Premier League?

As the English season entered its final stretch, every match was a must-win now for Liverpool, and Darwin was desperate to play his part.

Burnley at home? Yes, he secured the victory with a late header.

Brentford away? Yes, he opened the scoring with a cheeky chip on the counter-attack.

Luton at home? Darwin missed the match through injury, but his teammates got the job done without him.

Nottingham Forest away? He was back on the bench, and came on to head in the winner in the 99th minute!

'Yessssssssssss!' Darwin roared like the big lion tattoo on his back as he stood in front of the fans by the corner flag. It was his 10th league goal of the season and his most significant by far. Why? Because that win put Liverpool top of the table: one point ahead of Manchester City, and two ahead of Arsenal.

Ooooooooh, so close! Yes, for the first time in years, it was all set to be a super-exciting three-team title race...

Or was it? While Arsenal and Manchester City kept calm and carried on winning, Liverpool sadly stumbled and fell behind. The bad run began with a disappointing 2–2 draw with Manchester United, but it was the defeats against Crystal Palace and then their local rivals Everton that really ended their title hopes.

When the final whistle blew in the Merseyside Derby, Darwin was furious: with the referee, with his teammates, with his manager, but mainly with himself. He had started in both of Liverpool's big losses, and he had failed to take his big chances like a superstar striker should.

Against Palace, the ball had dropped perfectly for him just outside the six-yard box, but he had smashed his shot straight at the keeper. And a similar thing had happened against Everton too. When Mo slipped him through for a one-on-one, Darwin went for power instead of placement, and blasted the ball straight at the keeper again.

Arghhh, it was so frustrating! Earlier in the season, he had managed to keep calm and score just like Klopp had told him to, but now with the pressure on and the Premier League title on the line, he had lost his cool again.

After that Merseyside Derby defeat, things fizzled out for Liverpool and for Darwin. He came off the bench in their last four league games, but unfortunately there were no more super sub moments.

Oh well, despite the disappointing ending, it had still been a strong second season for Darwin:

1 trophy – the League Cup – his first major one for Liverpool,

Plus 18 goals and 13 assists.

That was already a big improvement on the previous year, and Darwin had the potential to do so much more. With his incredible pace and power, he was causing all kinds of problems for defenders and getting into all the right positions. Now, if he could just become more calm, clinical and consistent in front of goal, then he could easily double his numbers next season!

'I can do this,' Darwin told himself with the same determination as ever.

From his difficult early days in Artigas, he had fought his way to the top team in Uruguay; from injury hell, he had bounced back to become an even better footballer; and then from Spain's second division he had risen all the way to the UEFA Champions League and the Premier League.

So, for his next challenge? Darwin was going to prove his doubters wrong yet again and become Liverpool's leading goalscorer.

Read on for a sneak preview of
another brilliant football story by
Matt and Tom Oldfield. . .

ALISSON

Available now!

CHAPTER 1

CLUB CHAMPIONS OF THE WORLD!

21 December 2019, Khalifa International Stadium, Doha

What a year 2019 was turning out to be for Liverpool. The Reds were already the Champions of Europe, and now they were just one win away from becoming Champions of the World! Despite the club's amazing history, that was a title that they had never achieved before. The players were all really looking forward to competing in the 2019 FIFA Club World Cup Final – especially their great goalkeeper, Alisson.

As a boy growing up in Brazil, Alisson had watched his local team, Internacional, beat the mighty

Barcelona to win the tournament in 2006. What a proud and exciting night it had been! He had never forgotten that glorious victory over Ronaldinho and Co, and the way it made him feel as a fan. Ever since then, Alisson had dreamed of lifting that glittering gold trophy himself. Now his opportunity had arrived, and he was ready to catch it in his safe hands and never let go.

'Let's do this!' He clapped and cheered as the two teams emerged onto the pitch in Qatar.

To make things even more exciting for Alisson, Liverpool's opponents in the final were Flamengo, a club from Brazil. And in the Flamengo line-up, there were lots of familiar faces – his old Roma pal Gerson Santos da Silva, plus his national teammates Filipe Luís, Gabriel Barbosa, Diego Alves, Rodrigo Caio...

'Come on, we can't lose to this lot!' Alisson urged his defenders. That fighting spirit, developed all those years ago during his battles with brother Muriel, was what made him such a winner.

Trent Alexander-Arnold, Virgil van Dijk, Joe Gomez, Andy Robertson... Liverpool had the best back four in the business. But if Flamengo's attackers did somehow manage to get past them, Alisson would be there to save the day as usual.

For the first fifty minutes, however, he didn't have much shot-stopping to do. Liverpool were a team on the attack and their other Brazilian player, Roberto Firmino, missed two great chances to score. He blazed the first one over the bar and then hit the post with the second.

'So close!' Alisson groaned, standing on the edge of his area with his hands on his head.

Even though most of the action was happening at the other end of the pitch, Alisson always stayed alert. He couldn't let his concentration slip, not even for a second. Because as a keeper, you never knew when the ball would come flying towards you...

Suddenly, Éverton Ribeiro flicked it through to Barbosa, who turned and BANG! His shot was travelling towards the bottom corner, but down dived Alisson to push it powerfully away. SAVED!

What would Liverpool do without their calm and incredible keeper? As he got back up, Alisson was already organising his defenders for the corner. He wanted to win that FIFA Club World Cup trophy badly, and a clean sheet would be a lovely bonus.

Alisson was looking unbeatable, but unfortunately so was Diego Alves, the keeper at the other end. After ninety minutes, it was still 0–0. Would there be a winner in extra-time, or would Liverpool need a spot-kick king for a penalty shoot-out?

At last, a goal arrived. The captain Jordan Henderson played a perfect long pass to Sadio Mané, who squared it to Roberto inside the Flamengo box. Surely, he couldn't miss a hat-trick of chances? No, this time, he kept calm and hit the back of the net. 1–0 to Liverpool!

'Yessss!' Alisson punched the air with pride and passion, but he knew that the final wasn't over yet. No, they still had ten minutes of defending to do first, so they needed to…

'Focus!'

When the final whistle eventually blew, Alisson threw his arms up in the air and ran over to celebrate with his Liverpool family – Virgil van Dijk, his

ALISSON

manager Jürgen Klopp, and of course, Roberto. What
a year it had been for the two of them. They had won
the Champions League for their club, then the Copa
América for their country, and now this! Liverpool's
brilliant Brazilians kissed their latest trophy and
carried it proudly around the pitch.

'I'm really happy,' Alisson told the TV cameras,
with his winner's medal around his neck and his
gloves still on his hands. 'We won the Champions
League, and now we're in the race for the Premier
League again. But first, we need to enjoy this moment
– we're Club Champions of the World!'

DARWIN NÚÑEZ

Peñarol

🏆 Uruguayan Primera División: 2017, 2018

Liverpool

🏆 FA Community Shield: 2022

🏆 EFL Cup: 2023–24

Individual

🏆 LPFP Primeira Liga Player of the Year: 2021–22

🏆 Primeira Liga Top Scorer: 2021–22

🏆 Primeira Liga Team of the Year: 2021–22

NÚÑEZ

9

THE FACTS

NAME: Darwin Gabriel Núñez Ribeiro

DATE OF BIRTH: 24 June 1999

PLACE OF BIRTH: Artigas

NATIONALITY: Uruguay

BEST FRIENDS: His brother Junior

CURRENT CLUB: Liverpool

POSITION: ST

THE STATS

Height (cm):	187
Club appearances:	235
Club goals:	101
Club trophies:	4
International appearances:	22
International goals:	8
International trophies:	0
Ballon d'Ors:	0

★ ★ ★ **HERO RATING: 86** ★ ★ ★

GREATEST MOMENTS

24TH MAY 2019, URUGUAY 3–1 NORWAY

In this game at the 2019 FIFA U-20 World Cup in Poland, Darwin faced Erling Haaland for the first time and came out on top in the battle of the new young big guys. In the 21st minute, he chested a long ball down, let it bounce once, and then whipped a swerving shot over the keeper's head. Wow, Uruguay's next star striker had arrived!

2 — 14TH JULY 2019, PEÑAROL 4–0 BOSTON RIVER

After shining at the U-20 World Cup, this was the day Darwin hit top form for his club team too. Having previously only scored once in his first 14 games for Peñarol, here he grabbed a hat-trick in just 65 minutes! A tall striker with explosive pace and power, plus a good eye for goal – it wasn't long before Europe came calling...

3 — 16TH OCTOBER 2019, PERU 1–1 URUGUAY

In his first game for the Uruguay senior team, Darwin only entered the field as a late substitute, but within five minutes, he had already scored his first international goal. As Matías Viña curled a cross into the box, Darwin made a late dash to the front post and threw himself forward for a diving header, which landed in the bottom corner. Talk about a dream debut, eh?

4

15TH MARCH 2022,
AJAX 0–1 BENFICA

In his superstar second season at Benfica, Darwin just couldn't stop scoring, but this was probably his most important goal of all. After strikes against Barcelona and Bayern Munich in the group stage, he scored with a powerful flick header to send Benfica into the Champions League quarter-finals for the first time since 2016. Darwin had successfully caught the eye of clubs all over Europe.

5

30TH JULY 2022,
LIVERPOOL 3–1 MANCHESTER CITY

Following his record move to Liverpool, Darwin made his debut in this FA Community Shield against rivals Manchester City. Once more, he faced Haaland, and once more, he won the battle of the big guys. Darwin only came on in the 60th minute, but he completely changed the game. First, he helped win a penalty, and then he scored a goal of his own to secure the win and his first trophy in England.

TEST YOUR KNOWLEDGE

QUESTIONS

1. When Darwin was growing up, what was the main problem that his family faced in their neighbourhood of El Pirata?

2. Name at least three of Darwin's Uruguay heroes from the 2010 FIFA World Cup.

3. How old was Darwin when he tore his ACL at Peñarol?

4. What heroic thing did Junior do to help his brother Darwin?

5. Which future Premier League rival did Darwin face at the FIFA U-20 World Cup in Poland?

6. Which Spanish club did Darwin sign for in August 2019?

7. True or false – Darwin scored on his debut for the Uruguay national team?

8. Who recommended Darwin to Barcelona in Summer 2020?

9. How many goals did Darwin score for Benfica during the 2021–22 Primeira Liga season?

10. What happened to Darwin during his first Premier League home game for Liverpool against Crystal Palace?

11. For the 2023–24 season, Darwin took over the Liverpool Number 9 shirt from which club legend?

Answers below . . . No cheating!

1. *Flooding.* **2.** *Any of: Fernando Muslera, Diego Lugano, Diego Godín, Diego Forlán, Edinson Cavani, Luis Suárez, Nicolás Lodeiro* **3.** *17.* **4.** *Junior went home to look after the family and left Darwin to follow his professional football dream.* **5.** *Erling Haaland.* **6.** *Almería.* **7.** *True!* **8.** *His Uruguay hero and teammate Luis Suárez.* **9.** *26, in just 29 games.* **10.** *He was sent off for a head-butt.* **11.** *Roberto Firmino.*

PLAY LIKE YOUR HEROES

HOW TO LAUNCH A LIGHTNING-QUICK COUNTER-ATTACK LIKE DARWIN NÚÑEZ

STEP 1: First things first: even though you're an attacker, don't forget to do your defensive work too! Winning is one big team effort, but while you're back helping out, always stay alert for the sudden breakaway...

STEP 2: As soon as your team wins the ball back, it's time to go, go, go! Sprint forward up the pitch as fast as you can.

STEP 3: Don't just race off in any old direction, though; no, you've got to think smart out there! If your defender has launched a long ball forward, you'll probably want to just chase after it, but if one of your teammates is on the dribble, then you need to be somewhere else, in lots of space, ready to receive the pass...

STEP 4: When it comes towards you, stay calm and stay onside. Take a good first touch and get your head up and look around.

STEP 5: Is there still a defender in your way? If so, it might be best to pass the ball on to a teammate in a better position. But if not, keep going, keep cool, and make sure you win that 1-v-1 with the keeper...

STEP 6: GOAL! Hopefully you've still got enough energy left for a knee-slide in front of the fans.